THE SECRET OF SHAKESPEARE

S0-ARO-427

By the same author

ANCIENT BELIEFS AND MODERN SUPERSTITIONS
THE BOOK OF CERTAINTY
THE ELEMENTS AND OTHER POEMS
THE HERALDS AND OTHER POEMS
MUHAMMAD
THE QURANIC ART OF CALLIGRAPHY AND ILLUMINATION
A SUFI SAINT OF THE TWENTIETH CENTURY
WHAT IS SUFISM?

We shall presumably never know exactly how Shakespeare looked; but there is no doubt that the Droeshout engraving, published in the First Folio, has become the generally accepted image of the Bard. Blake's portrait – reproduced on the front cover – is recognizably derived from it, and we think that Blake would have applauded the contents of this book; but since his portrait is not the author's choice, we give here as a frontispiece what he, the author, considers to be 'possibly the truest visible impression of Shakespeare that we possess'. It is from a recent anonymous drawing based on the Droeshout engraving with reference to the Stratford bust and the Chandos portrait.

The Publishers

THE
SECRET OF
SHAKESPEARE

by

Martin Lings

Inner Traditions International
New York

Inner Traditions International Ltd.
377 Park Avenue South
New York, New York 10016

U.K. Edition published by Aquarian Press

All rights reserved. No part of this book may be reproduced or utilized in any form or by any means, electronic or mechanical, including photocopying, recording or by any information storage and retrieval system, without permission in writing from the Publisher. Inquiries should be addressed to Inner Traditions.

Library of Congress Cataloging in Publication Data

Lings, Martin.
    The secret of Shakespeare.

    Includes index.
    1. Shakespeare, William, 1564-1616 — Criticism and
Interpretation. I. Title.
PR2976.L465 1984   822.3'3   83-27300
ISBN 0-89281-059-9

Printed and Bound in Great Britain by
Whitstable Litho Ltd., Whitstable, Kent

Contents

The Earl of Gloster (blind)
The trick of that voice I do well remember.
Is't not the king? . . . O, let me kiss that hand.

King Lear (mad)
Let me wipe it first; it smells of mortality.

King Lear, IV, 6.

PREFACE

The title this book now bears in its second edition is the title round which the original manuscript was written. For the first edition it was changed for fear that false conclusions might be drawn from it about the contents. Lest these fears should now prove true, let it be clearly understood that the word 'secret' has nothing to do with any question of identity. The author believes William Shakespeare of Stratford-on-Avon to be in fact the artist of the works attributed to him. Most lovers of these works are of the same opinion. But many of them are none the less conscious of being faced by a certain enigma, difficult to define. Let us hope that these pages will provide them with a convincing solution.

What is the nature of this enigma? Is it the meagreness of our biographical knowledge that has conjured up the aura of mystery that surrounds Shakespeare? The answer is almost certainly no, for even if we were to discover a multitude of new facts about his life, that aura would still remain inviolate. It is not generated by our ignorance, but by what we know, namely his plays, or to be more precise, the plays of his maturity. It may well be, however, that this deeper mystery is not altogether unconnected with our general lack of information about the dramatist himself. The fact that apart from his writings he slipped through life so unobtrusively could well be considered as a characteristic feature of the particular greatness which this book claims for him.

Shakespeare has been defined more than once as 'the most famous writer in the world'. Admittedly, fame does not coincide with excellence; but he is by common consent – we might even say international consent – a dramatist who has never been surpassed, and in addition to his dramatic poetry, parts of which are highly lyrical, he is also supreme as a lyric poet in the double capacity of song-writer and sonneteer, while in a totally different domain he is a by-word as a portrayer of character, achieving by a few brilliant strokes of the pen what most novelists fail to achieve in a full-length novel. But to say all this, if it were merely this, would be to fall far short of his due; for wherever a certain level has been reached in art there are two greatnesses to be considered, not only that of the artist but also that of the man himself.

Shakespeare's greatness as an artist lies above all in the total impact that each of his best plays makes upon us when acted. But being a synthesis, this impact is not easily put into words; and once the curtain is down and we have left the theatre, what is said or written tends to do little justice to what we have experienced, and seems unable to account for it.

This book begins and ends with the mystery of the total impact, to which the title is closely related; but the secret in question has also an aspect which belongs to Shakespeare's greatness as a man – a greatness which, we maintain, is unmistakenly visible through the semi-transparent veil of his plays.

Martin Lings
London
1983

CHAPTER 1

SACRED ART

In the last few decades there has been a considerable increase of interest in the Middle Ages, which is no doubt partly due to a reaction, but it is also, much more, a case of ignorance giving way to knowledge. In another sense, it is simply a rising to the surface of something that has always been there and is always being rediscovered. Could it not be said that wherever the Middle Ages have not ceased to be accessible, wherever despite the barrier of the Renaissance they have always remained with us, as in the poetry of Dante, for instance, or – to take a more immediately accessible and inescapable example – as in their architecture, their superiority has always been felt at heart? This feeling implies also, if only subconsciously, the acknowledgement of a more general superiority, for it is quite impossible that the great Norman and Gothic cathedrals should have sprung from an age that had no inward excellence to correspond to these superlative outward manifestations.

One of the particular reasons for the present increase of interest in the Middle Ages is in itself highly significant: during the last fifty years Europeans have taken much more interest in the art of other civilizations than ever before, and this has no doubt uprooted many prejudices and opened the door to a certain freshness and objectivity of judgement. Having come to know some of the best examples of Hindu, Chinese and Japanese art and then as it were returning to their own civilization, many people find that their outlook has irrevocably changed. After looking at a great Chinese landscape, for example, where this world appears like a veil of illusion beyond which, almost visibly, lies the Infinite and Eternal Reality, or after having been given a glimpse of that same Reality through a statue of the Buddha, they find it difficult to take seriously a painting such as Raphael's famous Madonna, or Michelangelo's fresco of the Creation, not to speak of his sculpture, and Leonardo also fails to satisfy them. But they find that they *can* take very seriously, more seriously than before, some of the early Sienese paintings such as Lippo Memmi's Annunciation, for example, or the statuary and stained glass of Chartres Cathedral, or the twelfth- and thirteenth-century mosaics in St Mark's at Venice, or the icons of the Orthodox Church.

The reason why medieval art can bear comparison with Oriental art as no other Western art can is undoubtedly that the medieval outlook, like that of the Oriental civilizations, was intellectual. It considered this world above all as the shadow or symbol of the next, man as the shadow or symbol of God; and such an attitude, to be operative, presupposes the presence of intellectuals, for earthly things can only be referred back to their spiritual archetypes through the faculty of intellectual perception, the insight which pierces through the symbol to the universal reality that lies beyond. In the theocratic civilizations, if an artist himself was not an intellectual, he none the less obeyed the canons of art which had been established on an intellectual basis.

Sacred art in the full sense of the term is art which conforms to canons laid down not by individuals but by the spiritual authority of the civilization in question, as was the case with medieval Christian architecture, Gregorian chant, ancient Greek drama, Japanese No plays, Hindu temple dancing and music – to name only a few examples – and such art is always something of a criterion and also a potential source of inspiration for other less central works of art.

A medieval portrait is above all a portrait of the Spirit shining from behind a human veil. In other words, it is as a window opening from the particular on to the universal, and while being enshrined in its own age and civilization as eminently typical of a particular period and place, it has at the same time, in virtue of this opening, something that is neither of the East nor of the West, nor of any one age more than another.

If Renaissance art lacks an opening onto the universal and is altogether imprisoned in its own epoch, this is because its outlook is humanistic; and humanism, which is a revolt of the reason against the intellect, considers man and other earthly objects entirely for their own sakes as if nothing lay behind them. In painting the Creation, for example, Michelangelo treats Adam not as a symbol but as an independent reality; and since he does not paint in the image of God, the inevitable result is that he paints God in the image of man. There is more divinity underlying Simone Martini's painting of Saint Francis than there is in Michelangelo's representation of the Creator Himself.

Shakespeare was born less than three months after Michelangelo's death, and the two are often spoken of in the same breath as being among 'the greatest geniuses of the Renaissance'. Yet how does Shakespeare stand in the light of an intellectual approach which enhances, if possible, our respect for Dante, but which greatly diminishes our estimate of several others whose pre-eminence had long gone unquestioned? The following chapters are an attempt to answer this question in some detail; but a general answer can be given immediately. Let us quote, as touchstone, a masterly summing up of the difference between Renaissance art and medieval art: 'When standing in front of a Romanesque or Gothic cathedral, we feel that we are at the centre of the world; when standing in front of a Renaissance, Baroque or Rococo church we are merely conscious of being in Europe'.[1] Now without trying to give Shakespeare so essential a place in the art of Christendom as the place which is held by the medieval cathedrals or by *The Divine Comedy*, could it not be said that to be present at an adequate performance of *King Lear* is not merely to watch a play but to witness, mysteriously, the whole history of mankind?

But this remark could not possibly be made about the majority of Shakespeare's writings, and if we wish to form any estimate of the mature dramatist whose outlook bestowed on him a universality that is a prolongation of the universality of the Middle Ages, the first thing to be done is to set most of the plays on one side for the moment so as not to confuse the issue. Few writers can have developed so much during their period of authorship as Shakespeare did. By the end of the sixteenth century he had written some twenty-two plays; but none of these can be said to represent his maturity, though some of them,[2] in various ways, give an unmistakable foretaste of what was to come.

There can no longer be any doubt that already at the age of thirty[3] or before, Shakespeare was familiar with the various doctrines – some truly esoteric, others merely occultist – which so passionately interested the London dramatists and other writers of the day, as well as the aristocrats who sustained, protected and encouraged them, including two successive

1 Frithjof Schuon, *The Transcendent Unity of Religious* (Harper and Row, 1984) p.61, *note*.
2 *Romeo and Juliet*, for example, *A Midsummer Night's Dream, Henry IV, As You Like It*, and *Twelfth Night*.
3 In 1594; it was probably in this year that he wrote *Love's Labour's Lost*, and in the following year *Romeo and Juliet* and *A Midsummer Night's Dream*.

patrons[4] of the players for whom Shakespeare wrote his plays and with whom he acted. Needless to say, the mainstream of the mystical legacy of the Middle Ages was Christian; but by the end of the sixteenth century it had been swelled by many tributaries – Pythagorean, Platonic, Cabalistic, Hermetic, Illuminist, Rosicrucian, Alchemical. In the margin of some of these traditional currents were sciences such as astrology and magic, and many minds were captivated and even monopolized by side-issues of this kind.

But centrally, the non-Christian traditions coincided with Christian mysticism, despite differences of terminology and perspective. They were concerned firstly with the means of purifying the soul of its fallen nature, and finally with the fruit of that restoration of the primordial state, the soul's beatific reunion with God. Shakespeare, like Lyly, Spenser, Chapman and Ben Jonson – to name only a few – was well aware that the result of the chemical marriage of sulphur and quicksilver, or of 'the King and the Queen', the *magnum opus* of the Alchemists, is the perfected and resurrected soul, and that the alchemical work is thus an indispensable first stage on the path that leads finally to the mystic union of the perfect soul with the Divine Spirit. This union is in fact the theme of Shakespeare's alchemical poem *The Phoenix and the Turtle*, as Paul Arnold has demonstrated in his detailed commentary;[5] and if it be objected that this poem strikes too profound a note of maturity to be counted as a work of the mid nineties,[6] the same union, a marriage preceded and conditioned by trial and purification, is none the less the theme of more than one of Shakespeare's earlier plays. In this connection the reader has only to glance at Arnold's well-documented chapters on *Love's Labour's Lost* and *The Merchant of Venice*[7] or at Jean Paris's chapter on 'the alchemical theatre' in *Shakespeare*.[8]

The point to be made here is not that many of the earlier plays trace out symbolically the way of the Mysteries, but that they are too merely theoretical to be fully and 'concretely' mysterial. On the esoteric path doctrinal knowledge has to be acquired by the mind before it can be existentially assimilated by the man as a whole; and this process of development is outwardly reflected in the chronological order of the plays. It is one thing to make use of an assemblage of symbols, but it is

---

[4] See Paul Arnold, *Esotérisme de Shakespeare*, pp.60-1.
[5] *Ibid.*, pp.130-9.
[6] It was first published only in 1601.
[7] *Ibid.*, Chapters II and IV.
[8] Evergreen Books, 1960.

another thing to enter into that symbolism totally.

Let us suppose, to bring home our meaning, that Shakespeare had not lived to reach his maturity, or, in other words, that we had to build our estimate of his greatness on the basis of *Romeo and Juliet, A Midsummer Night's Dream, The Merchant of Venice, Richard II, Henry IV, Much Ado About Nothing, As You Like It, Julius Caesar* and *Twelfth Night,* these being probably the best of his earlier plays. The difference between that estimate and the one we are happily able to make would differ considerably from judge to judge, but it could not fail in any case to be vast. For it was only after these plays had been written, that is, just after the turn of the century, that there came a sharp and lasting change, not in orientation but in intensity. It was as if Shakespeare had suddenly come to grips with the universe after having contemplated it for some time with a half-detached serenity. From being in earnest, he had come to be in very deadly earnest. This change is forced on our attention first of all by *Hamlet*; and except for one or two backward glances, mostly in the direction of *Romeo and Juliet* and *Henry IV,* the scope of this book lies inclusively between *Hamlet* and Shakespeare's last complete play, *The Tempest.*

CHAPTER 2

SHAKESPEARE'S OUTLOOK

It is too often said that the marvellous variety of Shakespeare's characters makes it impossible to divine anything about the author himself. About his temperament this may be true to a certain extent, but as regards his outlook and ideals it is altogether false. We can learn much about him indirectly even from his villians, and from his heroes we can learn much more, especially towards the end of a play, after he has fully developed them.

But when the hero, in a manifest state of undevelopment, at the beginning or in the middle of a play, gives vent to his ideas about this and that, he is perhaps revealing his own immaturity and may well even be saying the very opposite of what Shakespeare himself thinks. A striking example of this is in *King Lear* when Gloster, who has an important part in the sub-plot, says, before Shakespeare has fully developed him:

> As flies to wanton boys, are we to the Gods;
> They kill us for their sport. (IV, 1)

It is when Edgar hears these words that he decides to set upon his strange course of action for the purpose of saving his father from despair and suicide. Thanks to his efforts, Gloster is able to say eventually:

> henceforth I'll bear
> Affliction till it do cry out itself
> 'Enough, enough', and die. (IV, 6)

and later still:

You ever-gentle Gods, take my breath from me:
Let not my worser spirit tempt me again
To die before you please!   (ibid.)

Now the great weakness of Gloster which he eventually overcomes, is akin to one of the weaknesses of Hamlet which he also overcomes, and which is lack of faith in Providence. The 'To be or not to be' soliloquy, from which so much has been deduced about Shakespeare's own views, does not merely not express the maturity of Hamlet but it shows him at his most immature, for in a sense the Prince goes back in development after the beginning of the play before he begins to go forward. When this particular soliloquy comes his faith is at its lowest ebb. Having more or less said at the beginning of the play that he would commit suicide if only God had not forbidden it, he now implies that he would do so but for *the dread of something after death*.

It is always possible that Shakespeare may have drawn on his own past experience for this soliloquy. But we can be certain that it does not represent in any way his settled convictions because its whole tenor is completely contradicted in the last scene of the play by the fully developed, perfectly balanced Hamlet voicing the maturity which Shakespeare has gradually shaped and built up for him. In this scene we find that he has altogether overcome his doubts. His now full-grown royalty of nature causes Horatio to exclaim, half in admiration, half in surprise: *'Why, what a king is this!'*; and his faith in Providence is unshakeable. He says to Horatio:

There's a divinity that shapes our ends,
Rough-hew them how we will.

This conversation leads up to what is perhaps the greatest speech of the play, though it is seldom quoted, partly no doubt because it is in prose. Hamlet's fencing match with Laertes is about to take place. Hamlet tells Horatio that he is confident of victory; yet at the same time he has a premonition that he is going to die, and he intimates as much to Horatio, who begs to be allowed to postpone the match. But Hamlet will not allow this. He says:

Not a whit, we defy augury: there's a special
providence in the fall of a sparrow. If it be
now, 'tis not to come; if it be not to come, it
will be now; if it be not now, yet it will come:
the readiness is all. Since no man has aught
of what he leaves, what is't to leave betimes?
Let be.

The gist of this speech, *the readiness is all*, is repeated almost word for word in an equally significant passage in the last act of *King Lear*. The news of the defeat and capture of King Lear and Cordelia plunges Gloster once more into despair. Edgar pulls him out of it by reminding him that just as a man has to submit to Providence as regards the time and manner of his birth, so also he must submit as regards the time and manner of his death and not seek to pluck the fruit before it is ripe.

> *Men must endure*
> *Their going hence, even as their coming hither.*
> *Ripeness is all.*

It will be noticed that in these two speeches of Hamlet and Edgar, as also elsewhere, Shakespeare is concentrating on the most universal aspect of religion. He is concerned with man's having the right attitude of soul towards Providence rather than with any particular mode of worship. But this does not mean that he himself was not a devout practising Christian. It simply means that in the extreme religious soreness and sensitivity of sixteenth and seventeenth century England, Christianity was a very dangerous topic. Before the end of his period of authorship it was even forbidden by law to mention the name of God on the stage. But one could always refer to 'the gods'; and if he deliberately chose to set many of his maturer plays in a pre-Christian setting, it is to be noticed none the less that his attitude to Greece and Rome is not typical of the Renaissance. He does not merely borrow the surface of classical antiquity. He places himself at the very centre of the ancient world. For him, and for Dante, just as for the ancient priests and priestesses at Delphi, Apollo is not the god of light but the Light of God.

In the form of his drama Shakespeare belongs to his age. Marlowe's *Dr Faustus* is outwardly in some respects more medieval than anything Shakespeare wrote. But in outlook Marlowe was altogether a man of the Renaissance, as were Ben Jonson and Webster, whereas Shakespeare seems in a sense to go back as time goes forward and by the turn of the century he had become, unlike any of his fellow dramatists, the continuer and the summer-up of the past, the last outpost of a quickly vanishing age. To say this is not really to say anything new; it is rather a case of putting two and two together. Bradley says of *King Lear:* 'It does not appear to disclose a mode of imagination so very far removed from the mode with which we must remember that Shakespeare was perfectly familiar in the Morality plays and in *The Faerie Queene.*' Of *Othello* Wilson Knight says: 'Othello, Desdemona and Iago are Man, the

Divine and the Devil', and he remarks in general that Shakespeare's heroes are 'purgatorial pilgrims'. Of *Macbeth* Dover Wilson says: '*Macbeth* is almost a morality play', and he says much the same of the two parts of *Henry IV*. Moreover, in this last connection, and with regard to Shakespeare as a continuer of past tradition, he reminds us: 'Before its final secularization in the first half of the sixteenth century, our drama was concerned with one topic and one topic only: human salvation. It was a topic that could be represented in either of two ways: (i) historically, by means of miracle plays which in the Corpus Christi cycles unrolled before the spectators' eyes the whole scheme of salvation from the Creation to the Last Judgement; or (ii) allegorically, by means of morality plays, which exhibited the process of salvation in the individual soul on its road between birth and death, beset with the snares of the World or the wiles of the Evil One.'[1] Dover Wilson does not define the word 'salvation' and for the purpose of his book, it is not necessary to do so. But as regards medieval art in general, it is important to distinguish between what may be called esoteric works, which look beyond salvation to sanctification, and exoteric works, in which sanctification is at best no more than a remote ideal. If Shakespeare is a continuer of the past, which of these two categories does his art belong to, the exoteric or the esoteric?

An example of what may be called an exoteric work which stops short at salvation in the lowest sense is *The Castle of Perseverance*. In this morality play mankind (*humanum genus*) is represented as having led a very questionable life, and he is saved from Hell in the face of justice by operation of the Divine Mercy. A supreme example of an esoteric work is *The Divine Comedy* which presupposes salvation and deals with man's purification and his ultimate sanctification or in other words his regaining of what was lost at the Fall. It may be said that in the Middle Ages the mass of the laity was considered as following the path of salvation, whereas the monastic orders, and the lay orders attached to them, and one or two other brotherhoods such as those of the Freemasons and the Companions, aimed at following the path of sanctification. In other words they aimed at passing through Purgatory in this life. It is now known that Dante belonged to a brotherhood which was affiliated to the Order of the Temple,[2] and which was more or less driven underground when the Order of the Temple was abolished.

[1] *The Fortunes of Falstaff*, Cambridge University Press, 1964, p.17.
[2] See René Guénon, *L'Ésotérisme de Dante* (Gallimard, 1957, p.11).

Some have supposed that Shakespeare was a member of the brotherhood of the Rosie Crosse; others believe him to have been a Freemason. This is a part of his secret which will probably never be known, and in any case it is not within the scope of these pages to dwell on anything that is not obvious from what he wrote. What *is* obvious, however, is that his plays far transcend the idea of salvation in its more limited sense; and it may be remarked in passing that this does suggest that their author was following a spiritual path, which itself implies attachment to an order.

At the beginning of Act V of *The Winter's Tale*, with reference to the long penance done by King Leontes during the sixteen years which elapse between the two parts of the play, the priestlike Cleomenes says:

> *Sir, you have done enough, and have perform'd*
> *A saint-like sorrow: no fault could you make*
> *Which you have not redeem'd; indeed, paid down*
> *More penitence than done trespass. At the last,*
> *Do as the heavens have done, forget your evil;*
> *With them forgive yourself.*

In *King Lear* the blind Gloster, recognizing the King's voice, asks to kiss his hand. Lear replies:

> *Let me wipe it first; it smells of mortality.*

This remark contains not only the very essence of the play but also of most of Shakespeare's other maturer plays; for in the course of them what does Shakespeare do but wipe away mortality, that is, the sin of Adam, from the hand of the hero? The hand must be altogether clean: there is no question of more or less. In *Hamlet* the prince says of himself in the middle of the play that he is fairly virtuous:

> *I am myself indifferent honest;*

but Shakespeare's purpose goes far beyond such mediocrity. The porter to the Gate of Purgatory, that is, the gate of salvation, is by definition of unfathomable mercy. Hamlet could have passed by him at the beginning of the play: so could Leontes at the moment of repentance, sixteen years before the speech just quoted; and so could Lear long before the end of the play. But the porter to the Gate of Paradise, that is, the gate to sanctification, is relentlessly exacting; and for his heroes and heroines, Shakespeare stands as that porter. He will let nothing pass except perfection; and so he makes Hamlet add to the above quoted words:

> *but yet I could accuse me of such things*
> *that it were better my mother had not born me.*

Character after character is developed to a state of virtue which is pushed, one feels, to the very limits of human nature, until each could say, with Cleopatra:

> *Give me my robe; put on my crown; I have*
> *Immortal longings in me.*

Even those who refuse to admit that Shakespeare himself speaks through any of his characters cannot escape from the fact that it is Shakespeare himself, and no one else, who is the architect of his plays. And when, after a certain maturity has been reached, play after play follows the same quest for human perfection, each play in its totality (over and above the marvellous variety of detail) hammering home the same message, we have no alternative but to conclude that Shakespeare was altogether preoccupied, at any rate for the last fifteen years of his life or more, by the same question which preoccupied Dante.

CHAPTER 3

HENRY IV

If *Hamlet* is Shakespeare's first really great play, the outlook which dominates it is none the less already to be found in several of his earlier plays. Particularly striking in this respect is *Henry IV* which, in its two parts, must have been written within three or four years before *Hamlet*, probably between 1597 and 1599.

Dover Wilson says: '*Henry IV* was certainly intended to convey a moral. It is, in fact, Shakespeare's great morality play.'[1] He adds:

Shakespeare plays no tricks with his audience . . . Prince Hal is the prodigal, and his repentance is not only to be taken seriously, it is to be admired and commended. Moreover the story of the prodigal, secularized and modernized as it might be, ran the same course as ever and contained the same three principal characters: the tempter, the younker, and the father with property to bequeath and counsel to give.[2]

This is altogether convincing, but it leaves unanswered the question as to whether the play is exoteric or esoteric. Or is it not in fact both? The idea of different meanings existing simultaneously at different levels, however strange it may seem to us, was altogether familiar to men of letters throughout the Middle Ages and even later – witness Spenser's *The Faerie Queene*.

According to Dante, 'writings are to be understood and should be expounded chiefly according to four meanings'[3] or in other words the

---

[1] *Ibid.*, p.14.
[2] *Ibid.*, p.22.
[3] *Il Convivio*, II, cap. 1.

literal meaning should be considered as a veil over three others, which
he specifies as 'allegorical, moral and anagogical'. The same principle is
to be found also in other arts: the idea that a true work of architecture
should have at least three meanings was certainly familiar to Freemasons
as late as the sixteenth century. A cathedral, in addition to its literal
meaning as a place of worship was planned as a symbolic image of the
whole universe, and by analogy, as an image of the human being,[4] both
body and soul. The symbolism of a building as an image of the human
soul, the inner world of man, corresponds to the fourth and highest
meaning mentioned by Dante, the one which he calls 'anagogical', and
which he illustrates by interpreting the Exodus of the Jews from Egypt
to the Promised Land to mean, in addition to its literal or historical
meaning, the exodus of the soul from the state of original sin to the state
of sanctification. Now this is also the highest or deepest meaning of the
story of the return of the Prodigal Son, and it could be said to underlie all
faithfully told stories of the prodigal, including Shakespeare's *Henry IV*,
even without the author's intention. But Shakespeare's intention is
undoubtedly there; we do not need to examine his text over carefully to
see that he conceived the newly crowned King Henry V's rejection of
Falstaff as representing more than salvation in the ordinary limited sense
of the word; for him it is clearly no less than the equivalent of the Red
Crosse Knight's victory over the dragon in *The Faerie Queene*; and this
victory, whatever else it may mean, clearly signifies above all the soul's
final purification, its final complete triumph over the devil.

We must be grateful to Dover Wilson for his timely reminder that
'Shakespeare lived in the world of Plato and St Augustine; since the
French Revolution we have been living in the world of Rousseau; and
this fact lays many traps of misunderstanding for unsuspecting readers.'[5]
He also says: 'The main theme of Shakespeare's morality play is the
growing up of a madcap prince into the ideal king.'[6] Putting two and two
together, it must be remembered that in the world of Plato and St
Augustine no man who was less than a saint could possibly pass as 'the
ideal king'.

No limit can be set to the extent of Prince Hal's reform. His world is
very remote indeed from the world we live in, the world of mediocrities

---

[4] For details of these correspondences see Titus Burckhardt, *Sacred Art in East and West*,
    p.45 (Perennial Books 1967).
[5] p.7.
[6] p.22.

and relativities in which epic is stifled beyond breathing point, while the psychological novel thrives and grows fat. There is an unmistakable ring of the absolute about the last scenes of *Henry IV*, which makes it difficult, from any point of view, to attribute to the new king anything that falls short of perfection. None the less this play can be said to have two meanings in relation to the human soul, one exoteric and moral, and the other esoteric and mystical; but as elsewhere in Shakespeare, these two meanings are not altogether distinct, for the lower meaning as it were opens on to the higher. *Henry IV* can be considered as a morality play in which the final perfection remains far above the spectators' heads, although it serves as a shrine of orientation for their ideals; and it can be considered as an esoteric or mystical drama, the purpose of which is to draw the spectator into the mesh of the plot, into the very person of the hero.

The meaning of *Henry IV* as a morality play is its literal meaning and needs no comment. As to its deeper meaning, one of the principal keys which the text offers us is the son's identification of himself with his dead father. A strange 'alchemy' has taken place by which the spirit of the old king is reborn in the person of the new king whose former faults – *affections* or *wildness* as he calls them – have died and lie buried with the old king.

> My father is gone wild into his grave,
> For in his tomb lie my affections,
> And sadly with his spirit I survive.   (Pt. 2, V, 2)

The young king also uses the image of the corrupt tide of vanity flowing out into the waters of the ocean so that a new and truly royal tide may flow in. Not far below the surface here, as elsewhere in Shakespeare's plays, lie the words of the Gospel 'Except a man be born again he cannot see the Kingdom of God'.

The heir's identification of himself with his father is important because in order to have a full understanding of *Henry IV* it is necessary to understand that 'Everyman' or the human soul is represented not merely by the Prince alone and by the King alone, but also, above all, by a synthesis of the Prince and the King. In its static aspect, as a fallen soul that 'smells of mortality' and must die before a new soul can be born, the soul is personified by the King; and the symbolism is strengthened by the fact that the King is a usurper to the throne, just as fallen man is a usurper to the throne of earth, which belongs by rights only to man in his original state, man created in the image of God. On the other hand, in its dynamic aspect, inasmuch as it is capable of being purified, and inasmuch as the foundations of the new soul are being laid there, the soul is personified by the Prince who, at any rate according to the logic of the play, will not be a usurper when he becomes King. It is not only the faults of the Prince that die with his father's death but also the stigma of a crown that had been usurped. The dying King says of his own wrongful seizure of the throne:

> All the soil of this achievement goes
> With me into the earth . . .
> How I came by the crown, O God forgive,
> And grant it may with thee in true peace live.   (IV, 5)

The substance of the soul of 'Everyman' is also represented by England, which is in a state of discord and which is gradually brought into a state of peace. The two plots of the play, the bringing to order of the Prince and the bringing to order of the country, run parallel to each other and have the same significance. Civil war is a most adequate symbol of the fallen soul, which is by definition at war with itself; and the meaning of this particular internal strife in England is heightened by the King's intention to convert its energies, as soon as possible, into a holy war. The whole play is in fact consecrated by beginning and ending, as it were, in the shadow of the Holy Land. At the beginning of Part I the King announces his intention of leading a crusade to Jerusalem; and towards the end of Part II he reaffirms this intention, announcing that all preparations have been made to set out for Palestine as soon as the rebels at home have been defeated:

> Now, Lords, if God doth give successful end
> To this debate that bleedeth at our doors
> We will our youth lead on to higher fields
> And draw no swords but what are sanctified.
> Our navy is address'd, our power collected,
> Our substitutes in absence well invested,
> And everything lies level to our wish.   (IV, 4)

The rebels have in fact already been defeated, but the news has not yet reached him. Symbolically connected with this is another 'already' which, though it dawns on him later, he has also not yet grasped: he is already in 'Jerusalem' – the Jerusalem Chamber of the Palace of Westminster where this scene takes place; and here, shortly after his just quoted speech, when news comes that the civil war is at an end, he suddenly sinks down in mortal sickness. For the moment the play's deeper meaning wells to the surface as it were and obliterates the other meanings. The only connection between the good news and the King's illness is a spiritual one: the end of the civil war means that the pilgrim's journey is at an end, that the old soul is now ripe for death so that the new soul may be born. If the King is no more than dying and not yet dead, this is simply because the return of his prodigal son has not yet been fulfilled. Once this has taken place the King asks to be carried back into the Jerusalem Chamber, in order that he may die *in Jerusalem*.

The Jerusalem Chamber has also its meaning for the Prince. We may remember that in *The Faerie Queene* the Red Crosse Knight is only able to overcome the dragon because the fight takes place at the threshold of the Earthly Paradise, within reach of the Waters of Life and the Tree of Life.[7] Now Jerusalem is symbolically equivalent to the Earthly Paradise; and the Prince's real victory over himself, when he speaks of

The noble change that I have purpos'd

takes place as he stands by his dying father's bed at the threshold of the Jerusalem Chamber, before his final meeting with Falstaff. This symbolism is strengthened by another; for if any particular moment can be assigned to the Prince's victory, it is at his foretaste of royalty when, believing himself to be by rights already king, he places the crown on his own head.

The last scenes of *Henry IV* Part II, make an undeniably strong spiritual impact. But neither part of *Henry IV*, when taken as a whole, has anything approaching the closely knit intensity of a play like *Hamlet*. In particular we cannot help noticing that there is no real conflict: like the killing of the dragon, the rejection of Falstaff symbolizes the most difficult thing in the world, and yet the Prince has not had, as far as we can see, the slightest difficulty in rejecting him. Secondly – and this weakness is connected with the first – Shakespeare makes the rejection of Falstaff very dramatic, but he has not previously brought home to us dramatically Falstaff's utter villainy. The villainy is there in the text, but we only discover it by analysis; the plot of the play does not depend on it at all, so that at the end we have a certain sense of disproportion which

---

[7] Spenser died in 1599, about the time that Shakespeare was writing this play. *The Faerie Queene*, which death prevented him from finishing, is mentioned here and elsewhere as an example of symbolism parallel to Shakespeare's at the end of the sixteenth century, without any claim that Spenser had a more than theoretic understanding of the symbolism that he was using.

leaves us with a vague feeling of injustice. But it may well be that we partly owe the excellence of some of Shakespeare's later plays to his experience in writing this. Perhaps when conceiving the part of Iago he said to himself, thinking of Falstaff: 'This time there shall be no mistake!'; and perhaps when he set Hamlet to kill the dragon he said to himself: 'This time it shall *not* be easy!'

CHAPTER 4

HAMLET

The basic theme of *Hamlet* is summed up in the Prince's own words:

> *Virtue cannot so inoculate our old stock*
> *but we shall relish of it.*   (III, 1)

This means: 'It is no use plastering one or two superficial virtues over our old stock, that is, the original sin which permeates our nature, since in spite of all such virtues, we shall still continue to reek of the old stock.' But in order to express fully what is in Hamlet's mind here we must add: 'There is only one thing which can effectively wipe out the stench of our old stock and that is *revenge*, or in other words a complete reversal of the state of affairs which caused the Fall.'

In its immediate impact upon us sacred art[1] is like a stone thrown into water. The ever widening ripples illustrate the limitless repercussions that are made, or can be made, upon the soul by this impact, fraught as it is with several meanings at different levels. One meaning can, as we have seen, open out on to another deeper meaning[2] that lies beyond it. In this way sacred art often conveys far more than it appears to convey, far more sometimes even than the mind in question is conscious of or could take in by way of ordinary didactic teaching.

Needless to say, the initial impact itself must captivate the mind and

---

[1] Shakespeare's plays cannot be considered as sacred art in the full and central sense of the term, but they can be considered as an extension of it, and as partaking both of its qualities and its function.

[2] Not that every detail in the text has a deeper meaning. Conversely, there are some details which only make good sense on the deepest plane of all.

the emotions. According to the literal meaning of *Hamlet*, our sense of Queen Gertrude's culpability goes far beyond the sin of marriage to a dead husband's brother, just as we are given many strong and obvious reasons why Hamlet should kill Claudius, enough at any rate even to make us forget for the moment that revenge is un-Christian. None the less, it would be true to say that there is no common measure between the literal meaning of this play and the deep sense of urgency that Shakespeare instils into us. There is something mysteriously unfathomable about the Queen's guilt. Moreover, so long as we are in the theatre we are not far from feeling that revenge is the most important thing in the world; and we are right, for there *is* nothing more important, and indeed nothing more Christian, than what revenge stands for here.

The Ghost's revelation to Hamlet is, as regards its symbolic meaning, like a puzzle with a few missing pieces which it is not difficult for us to supply in the light of those pieces which we are given – the garden with its fruit trees, the serpent, the guilty woman. The *Genesis* narrative is undoubtedly here. There is also, explicitly, the first-fruit of the Fall, the sin of fratricide.[3] But the Fall itself was in fact a murder also, the slaying or making mortal of Adam by the serpent, and the forbidden fruit was the 'poison' through which that murder was effected.

The Queen is not merely Hamlet's mother; she is his whole ancestral line going back to Eve herself; and inasmuch as she is Eve, she represents, in general, the fallen human soul, especially in its passive aspect. In other words, she represents that passivity which in man's primordial state was turned towards Heaven and which after it lost contact with the Spirit has come more or less under the sway of the devil or, in the words of the play, having *sated itself in a celestial bed* has come to *prey on garbage*. Like the father and son in *Henry IV*, mother and son here can each be taken separately as representing 'Everyman', but above all they are to be taken together as constituting the fallen human soul, Hamlet himself being the personification of its active aspect – its conscience and its intelligence. The attitude of the son towards his mother, which many people consider to be something of an enigma and which has prompted more than one grotesque explanation, is amply explained if we consider that allegorically mother and son are one person, different faculties of one and the same soul.

[3] The murderer himself says:

> Oh, my offence is rank, it smells to heaven;
> It hath the primal eldest curse upon't,
> A brother's murder! (III, 2)

Unlike the writer of epic, the dramatist has a very limited space at his disposal. Consequently, he often chooses to build a house of more than one storey. In *Hamlet* the soul is not only represented by the Prince and his mother; its state is also reflected in the condition of the country. Not that there is actually a sub-plot of civil war as in *Henry IV*, but none the less

> *Something is rotten in the state of Denmark*

and *The time is out of joint* and needs to be *set right*. Moreover, as a parallel to the whole action of the play, the soul of King Hamlet is being purified in Purgatory.

But the dead King has also another aspect. Just as Adam was not only the man who fell but also the most perfect of all creatures, made in the image of God, so also King Hamlet, who in a sense corresponds to Adam, is not only a purgatorial pilgrim but also a symbol of man's lost Edenic state. It is in virtue of this that he refers to his own marriage with Gertrude as a *celestial bed*, and is spoken of by Hamlet in terms of human perfection:

> *A combination and a form indeed*
> *Where every god did seem to set his seal*
> *To give the world assurance of a man.*   (III, 4)

It is also in virtue of this aspect that he acts as spiritual guide to his son.

The difference between simple piety and mysticism might almost be summed up by saying that the averagely pious man looks at the story of the Garden of Eden for the most part objectively, whether he takes it literally or allegorically. The mystic, on the other hand, looks at it subjectively as something which intensely, directly and presently concerns himself. Again, the averagely pious man is aware of the existence of the devil, but in fact, if not in theory, he imagines him to be more or less harmless and has little idea of the extent of his own subservience to him. In general he is extremely subject to the illusion of neutrality. But the mystic knows that most of what seems neutral is harmful, and that *one may smile and smile and be a villain*. The Ghost initiates Hamlet into the Mysteries by conveying to him the truth of the Fall not as a remote historical fact but as an immediate life-permeating reality, an acute pain which will not allow his soul a moment's rest; and every man in fact is in exactly the same situation as the Prince of Denmark, did he but know it, that is, if he were not?

Duller . . . than the fat weed
That roots itself at ease on Lethe wharf.   (I, 4)

What the Ghost says to Hamlet could almost be paraphrased:
'Latterly you have been feeling that *all is not well.* I come to confirm your
worst suspicions and to show you the remedy. Since man has been
robbed by the devil of his birthright, there is only one way for him to
regain what is lost and that is by taking revenge upon the robber.'

With all the ardour of the novice, in answer to his father's last
injunction *Remember me!* the Prince replies:

Remember thee?
Yea, from the table of my memory
I'll wipe away all trivial fond records,
All saws of books, all forms, all pressures past,
That youth and observation copied there;
And thy commandment all alone shall live
Within the book and volume of my brain,
Unmix'd with baser matter.   (I, 4)

Spiritual wisdom, from a worldly point of view, is a kind of madness;
and so madness can be made to serve, in certain contexts, as a symbol of
spiritual wisdom. Shakespeare avails himself of this possibility more
than once in his plays; and in *Hamlet*, in addition to its more outward
meaning as a stratagem and a blind, the *antic disposition* which the Prince
puts on serves above all to underline the drastic change that has taken
place in his life. In his soliloquies he shows no trace of madness; but as
soon as he has to face the world, that is, when Horatio and Marcellus
enter, shortly after the exit of the Ghost, the new found spiritual
outlook which fills his soul almost to bursting point has to find an outlet
in what Horatio describes as *wild and whirling words.* It is under cover of
this 'wildness' that Shakespeare momentarily allows the deeper meaning
of the play to come to the surface, for what Hamlet says is:

And so without more circumstance at all,
I hold it fit that we shake hands and part;
You, as your business and desire shall point you;
For everyman hath business and desire,
Such as it is; and, for mine own poor part,
Look you, I'll go pray.

And prayer, which in the widest sense of the word may be said to comprise all forms of worship, is in fact man's chief weapon of 'revenge'.[4]

It is not, however, Horatio and Marcellus who represent the world in *Hamlet*. They do so in this scene only incidentally, because they are the first living creatures that the newly initiated Prince is called upon to face. But he soon takes them both half into his confidence, and later he confides everything to Horatio. The world, not only in its incomprehension, but also in its allurements, everything in 'ordinary life' which it is difficult to give up but which the man who has taken his vows must break with altogether and leave behind is summed up in the person of Ophelia. Hamlet's subsequent visit to her, which she describes to her father, would seem to be prompted by the vain hope that it may not be necessary to turn his back on the world altogether, or that it may be possible as it were to take the world with him. But when he looks into her face he sees that he must go his way alone; she would be quite incapable of sharing his secret; and so he leaves her without saying a word.

In the 'nunnery scene', where we first see them together, Shakespeare once more allows the deeper meaning of the play to rise to the surface under cover of Hamlet's 'madness'. The first part of the spiritual path is 'the descent into Hell'. The deeper meaning of Dante's *Inferno*[5] is the descent of Dante into the hidden depths of his own soul. The novice has first to learn the meaning of 'original sin'; he must come to know the evil possibilities which lie, almost unsuspected, beneath the surface illusion of being *indifferent honest*. The gist of all that Hamlet says to Ophelia in this scene is in the following speech:

> *Get thee to a nunnery; why wouldst thou be a breeder*
> *of sinners? I am myself indifferent honest; but yet I could*
> *accuse me of such things that it were better my mother had not*
> *borne me. I am very proud, revengeful, ambitious; with more*

---

[4] The already quoted line:

> *Let me wipe it* [my hand] *first; it smells of mortality*

which brings the deeper meaning of *King Lear* to the surface, is spoken by Lear when he is mad. The fact that Hamlet's madness is feigned whereas Lear's is not makes no difference to its symbolism. Another kind of 'madness' which has the same significance is the 'folly' of the professional fool.

[5] The references here and elsewhere to Dante do not mean to suggest that Shakespeare owes anything to him directly. Of this we know nothing. *The Divine Comedy* can none the less help to throw light on certain aspects of these plays because it is based on principles with which no intellectual of Shakespeare's time could fail to be familiar.

offences at my beck than I have thoughts to put them in,
imagination to give them shape, or time to act them in. What
should such fellows as I do, crawling between heaven and earth?
We are arrant knaves all; believe none of us. Go thy ways to
a nunnery.   (III, 1)

Elsewhere 'the descent into Hell', that is, the discovery of sinful propensities in the soul which were hitherto unknown, takes the form of actually committing the sins in question, as happens, for example, with Angelo in *Measure for Measure* and with Leontes in *The Winter's Tale*. The same may be said also of Macbeth, but his 'descent', as we shall see, is of a different kind.

Despite Hamlet's *antic disposition*, all that he says to Ophelia in the 'nunnery scene' makes profound sense. But 'the world' is quite uncomprehending; for Ophelia it is all nothing more than

Sweet bells jangled, out of tune and harsh.

In *The Divine Comedy* the discovery of the soul's worst possibilities and purification from them are treated separately. The *Inferno* and the *Purgatorio* correspond to an altogether exhaustive Confession followed by a full Absolution. The 'architecture' of Dante's poem demands this separate treatment, as also the fact that it has an eschatological as well as a mystical meaning. Occasionally, as we shall see, Shakespeare also treats the two phases separately, but more often, as in *Hamlet*, he represents them as taking place simultaneously. The killing of Claudius will mean reaching not only the bottom of Hell but also the top of the Mountain of Purgatory, for revenge means purification.

When Hamlet, on his way to speak with his mother, suddenly comes upon Claudius praying and is about to kill him, he refrains from doing so on the grounds that to kill him while at prayer would amount to sending him to heaven, which would be *hire and salary, not revenge*. According to the more outward meaning, that is, according to *Hamlet* as a morality play, the Prince's failure to kill Claudius at this juncture springs from the inability to take decisive action, the readiness to snatch at any pretext for procrastination. At this level a more or less blind eye has to be turned to the actual pretext given. None the less, it is difficult to pass it over altogether as an unpremeditated excuse which flashes across Hamlet's mind and is seized on without being weighed, because later in the play Hamlet deliberately sends Rosencrantz and Guildenstern to a sudden death, *no shriving time allowed*, without even knowing whether they are in the plot against his life or not – and in all probability they are not. We can accept the normal idea of revenge without too much difficulty, even in a morality play, for revenge is or can be a name for justice. But what sin can compare with the implacable determination to send a soul to Hell?[6] And how is such appalling malevolence to be reconciled with the fact that Hamlet is unquestionably a man of great nobility and magnanimity of character, with a profound love of good and hatred of evil and with even much of the priest in his nature – witness the wise, benign and moving sermon he preaches to his mother in the next scene? It must be admitted, with regard to these questions, that the play's deeper meaning strains here the outward sense almost to breaking point. But once the deeper meaning is understood, the difficulties vanish. Revenge on the devil must be absolute. It requires no apologies. There must be no scruples and no compromise. But the time is not yet ripe. There would be no revenge, and therefore no self-purification, in killing Claudius at that moment because Claudius is not himself. Sometimes the soul's worst possibilities may manifest themselves only partially, in such a way that it would be quite easy to overcome them. But nothing final could be hoped for from resisting them on such an occasion; it is only when those possibilities really show themselves for what they are, when they are rampant in all their iniquity, only then is it possible, by stifling them, to give them the death-blow or mortally wound them. As Hamlet says:

> When he is drunk asleep, or in his rage,
> Or in the incestuous pleasure of his bed,
> At gaming, swearing, or about some act
> That has no relish of salvation in't;
> Then trip him, that his heels may kick at heaven
> And that his soul may be as damn'd and black
> As hell, whereto it goes.   (III, 3)

In this scene the devil is far from manifesting himself fully in Claudius. The dragon has not yet come out into the open. Or in other words,

---

[6] As answer to this question we may quote from *Measure for Measure* (written about the same time as *Hamlet*) what the Duke says about sending a soul to Hell. He has been trying to prepare Barnardine for death, a criminal justly sentenced to be executed for murder. When asked if Barnardine is ready to die, the Duke replies:

> A creature unprepared, unmeet for death;
> And to transport him in the mind he is
> Were damnable.   (IV, 3)

Hamlet has not nearly reached the bottom of Hell. He has not even had yet *any direct* experience of the full villainy of Claudius. All that he has learnt so far is relatively indirect compared, for example, with what he finds when he opens the letter to the King of England and reads Claudius' instructions to have him beheaded immediately on arrival; but the very bottom of Hell is only reached when the Queen lies dead and Hamlet's own body has tasted the poison. Meantime, before he can kill the great devil he has first of all to account for the lesser devils – Polonius, Rosencrantz and Guildenstern; and like Dante's 'cruelty' towards some of the sufferers he sees in Hell, who are really elements in his own soul, Hamlet's attitude becomes immediately understandable and acceptable and reconcilable with his nobility of nature if we realize that all the victims of his revenge are in a sense part of himself.

What has so far most impeded Hamlet upon his path is a certain apathy, sluggishness and lack of fervour. *Lapsed in time and passion* is the way he describes himself. The basic cause of this half-heartedness, the chief reason why it is out of the question that Claudius should be killed at this moment of the play, is that the soul is divided against itself, being still, in so far as it is represented by the Queen, largely under the Devil's domination. It is only in the next scene that a certain unity of soul is achieved when Hamlet wins his mother over to his side.

This scene is as it were the centre of the play. Personifying the soul that is afraid of its conscience, the Queen is afraid of her son and has been holding him at bay. Even now, when the two are to be alone together at last, she has contrived, or rather let us say, willingly consented, to have a third party present, one of the devil's spies, hiding behind the arras. Polonius is the embodiment of hypocrisy. His presence at the beginning of this scene means the presence, in the soul, of the determination to brazen things out. The Queen's first words to Hamlet, referring to Claudius as his 'father', are shameless in their effrontery:

> *Hamlet, thou hast thy father much offended.* (III, 4)

But when Hamlet's sword pierces the body of Polonius, conscience pierces through the soul's mask of self-justification and with all possibility of intervention at an end the soul is forced to listen to its better self:

> *Leave wringing of your hands. Peace, sit you down*
> *And let me wring your heart; for so I shall*
> *If it be made of penetrable stuff,*

> *If damned custom have not braz'd it so*
> *That it is proof and bulwark against sense.*

The Queen is eventually driven to say:

> *O Hamlet, speak no more!*
> *Thou turn'st mine eyes into my very soul;*
> *And there I see such black and grained spots*
> *As will not leave their tinct.* [7]

No sooner is the soul's repentance assured than its good angel appears. Gertrude, representing the lower part of the soul, cannot sense directly the spiritual power which the ghost of her dead husband represents; but Hamlet sees and hears it, and under its inspiration he tells his mother what she must do.

In this scene, which is really an epitome of the whole play, even the literal sense rises to heights that are almost mystical. It is as if the drama's outer meaning, in virtue of which it is a morality play, had been drawn up to the level of its inner meaning. For whether we consider the Prince to be addressing another person or to be addressing his own soul, he is in any case speaking with an exalted penetration worthy of a spiritual master who has years of practical experience of the mystic path behind him.

According to the First Quarto[8] version of this scene Hamlet succeeds in destroying once and for all Claudius' hold over Gertrude. Moreover she promises to help Hamlet to accomplish his revenge. This is left out of the masterly revised text of the Second Quarto,[9] which leaves the audience with the impression, not that Gertrude has completely conquered her weakness for Claudius but that she is well on her way to doing so and that she is sincerely repentant and determined to give her son all the passive support she can. They feel that, like Hamlet himself, she still has some obstacles to overcome; and indeed if she had not, and if Hamlet had not, Claudius would have to die then and there.

To judge from the cuts in the first Folio edition of *Hamlet*, published only seven years after Shakespeare's death, we may assume that the full text of this play was considered then, as now, too long for the requirements of theatrical performance. Unfortunately, one of the

---

[7] Nothing I can say to myself will make them leave their black tint to take on a lighter colour.

[8] 1603.

[9] 1604.

passages nearly always sacrificed is Act IV, scene 4, without which the balance of the play as a whole is seriously upset. In this scene Hamlet, on his way to the Danish coast to set sail for England, has a glimpse of Fortinbras, the young Prince of Norway, who is leading his army through Denmark to fight against the Poles; and this glimpse reveals to Hamlet a hero endowed with all those virtues which he himself most needs to develop.

Fallen man stands between two perfections, one past and one future, that which was lost and that which is to be gained. In this play it is the dead King Hamlet who stands for the past perfection and its loss, whereas Fortinbras represents the perfection in which the redeemed soul, after its purification, will be reborn. It is he whom the dying Hamlet is to name as his heir. The analogy between the symbolism of this play and that of *Henry IV* is by no means exact in every detail; but the dead King Hamlet largely corresponds to the dead King Richard II, whereas Queen Gertrude and her son, taken together, correspond to the the synthesis of King Henry IV and his son,[10] while Fortinbras in a sense corresponds to that son regenerated as King Henry V. But this scene, where Fortinbras first appears, is needed above all in that it marks a stage in the development of Hamlet, who drinks a new strength into his soul from his vision of Fortinbras. In the soliloquy which is prompted by his foretaste of his own true self there is a ring of confidence and resolution which we have not heard before. It must be remembered in this connection that the symbolism of honour throughout this play is inextricably connected with the symbolism of revenge. In other words, as the incentive to revenge, honour means spiritual aspiration.

In *Hamlet*, as also in *King Lear*, the play begins with worldly wisdom in a state of triumph. It is as if Shakespeare had set up a pair of scales, and to begin with he allows the weight of worldly wisdom in one scale to lift the opposite scale of spiritual wisdom right up into the air, so that it appears as 'light' as folly. But as the play goes on, more and more weight is thrown into the spiritual scale until, even before the last act, it has sunk down to rest on a solid, sober foundation. By the time *King Lear* is drawing to its close the Fool has disappeared, Edgar has ceased to feign

---

[10] Needless to say there is no exact correspondence here between parent and parent and between son and son. It is true that Gertrude is burdened with guilt towards King Hamlet just as Henry IV is burdened with guilt towards King Richard; but Prince Hamlet, the censurer of self and others, also has much in common with Henry IV, whereas Gertrude in some respects comes closer, symbolically, to the repentant prodigal Prince Hal.

madness, and Lear has recovered his sanity. Similarly, in *Hamlet* we see
no more of the Prince's 'madness' after he has left for England; and
when he returns he astonishes Horatio with his new-found strength and
determination. Meantime it is the scale of worldly wisdom which,
found sadly wanting, hangs poised aloft in insecure suspense; and the
'lightness' of this world, unstable and transitory as it is, racing towards
decay, ruin and death, is pictured in the madness of Ophelia. For her
there are only two categories – the dead and the dying.

> *And will he not come again?*
> *And will he not come again?*
> *No, no, he is dead.*
> *Go to thy death bed.*
> *He never will come again.*   (IV, 5)

Ophelia's madness is like a mirror for the failure of all worldly
aspirations, the shattering of all worldly hopes; and it is significant,
considering what she stands for in the play as a whole, that the corpse
which is being buried in the church-yard scene is none other than hers.

In this scene, Hamlet, who is himself to die the next day, has the
inevitable certainty of death brought home to him with a concrete
realism which makes his bones ache, and those of the audience too. He is
made to hear death in the knocking together of dead men's bones as the
grave-digger throws down one against another; he sees, touches and
smells death as he takes the jester's skull in his hands; he even almost
tastes death as he remembers how often as a child he had put his lips
against what is now no more than two rows of teeth set in two jaw-
bones:

> *Here hung those lips that I have kissed I*
> *know not how oft.*   (V, 1)

Moreover the scene is to end with the actual burial of everything that
had represented, for Hamlet, the possibility of earthly happiness.[11] His
own days are numbered too, for it comes out that the grave-digger had
taken up his profession on the day that Hamlet was born, thirty years
previously; and for him the Prince is already almost a thing of the past,
one who has not only come but gone. There is a strange and sudden chill

---

[11] There is a strong suggestion of death agony in the convulsive violence of Hamlet's
outburst over Ophelia's grave – his *towering passion* as he regretfully describes it the
next day.

about the words, spoken with the objectivity of a chronicle:

It was the very day that young Hamlet was born;
he that is mad, and sent into England.

We are reminded by this scene that more than one mystic has sought before now to familiarize himself with death by laying himself out in a coffin; and this is precisely what Hamlet is made to do here. It leads up to his speech in the final scene where he expresses his readiness to die at any time. What does it matter if a man die young, since no man really ever possesses any of the things he leaves behind him at death?

Since no man has aught of what
he leaves, what is't to leave betimes?

We have come a long way from the fears expressed about death in the most famous of his soliloquies.

That soliloquy, *To be or not to be . . .*, marks Hamlet's lowest ebb. As has already been pointed out in an earlier chapter, he goes somewhat back after the first encounter with his father before he begins to go forward. We cannot start to trace the development of the soul he represents until the play-scene, in which doubts are altogether removed and faith confirmed. Onwards from there, the soul gains singleness and sincerity from the reconciliation between Hamlet and his mother; confidence, resolution, a sense of true greatness and even a foretaste of perfection from the glimpse of Fortinbras; resignation to death and a foretaste of death from the churchyard scene; and complete trust in Providence from the discovery of Claudius' letter to the King of England. Hamlet's discovery of this plot to have him killed in England takes place shortly after he sees Fortinbras, but we only hear of it in the last scene of the play. He ascribes, with considerable insistence, every detail of his escape to Divine intervention, and his account of what happened enables trust in Providence to take its place as cornerstone in the remarkable image of royalty which Shakespeare gives us in Hamlet at the beginning of this scene. Without the least arrogance, but with an altogether objective sense of values, he dismisses Rosencrantz and Guildenstern as *baser natures* who have perished for daring to step between two *mighty opposites*, that is, between himself and Claudius – *mighty* because, as we may interpret, since all Heaven is on his side, as he now knows beyond doubt, the clash is ultimately between Michael and Lucifer.

Why, what a king is this!

exclaims Horatio in wonderment. It is significant also that only here, for the very first time, does Hamlet mention among Claudius' other iniquities, that he has robbed him of his rightful crown; and when Horatio implies that there is no time to be lost because news of what has happened will shortly come from England, and when Hamlet replies:

> *It will be short; the interim is mine;*
> *And a man's life's no more than to say 'One'*

we know that Claudius has not long to live.

The keynote of this opening passage to the final scene is maturity – readiness in every sense of the word, and it is summed up in the words *the readiness is all.* 'Everyman' knows that he has almost come to the end of his journey and that the end will be victory but also, necessarily, death. The confidence in the one and the foreboding of the other are expressed in Hamlet's words to Horatio:

> *I shall win at the odds. But thou*
> *wouldst not think how ill all's*
> *here about my heart.*

These words, with their combination of victory and death, are equivalent to Henry IV's:

> *And wherefore should these good news make me sick?*
> (IV, 4)

as he hears of his victory over the rebels. Symbolically the two situations are identical; Henry IV here corresponds exactly to Hamlet before the fencing match. All that remains to be achieved, in either case, is the complete redemption of the other aspect of the soul, represented in *Henry IV* by the Prince and in *Hamlet* by the Queen. As regards the Queen, 'the return of the prodigal' has in a sense already taken place; but art demands that it should be clinched beyond all doubt. In this respect, what is generally accepted today as the final text is almost certainly more elliptical than Shakespeare originally intended it to be when he conceived the play. After the King and Laertes withdraw together at the end of Act IV, scene 5, the First Quarto has a scene in which Horatio tells the Queen of Claudius' unsuccessful attempt to have Hamlet killed in England and of Hamlet's return. When the Queen learns that her son is back in Denmark, she tells Horatio:

Bid him awhile
Be wary of his presence, lest he fail
In that he goes about

which means, freely paraphrased: 'Tell him to make quite sure that Claudius does not kill him before he kills Claudius'. But although this scene is left out in all the later editions of the play, according to the final text a letter is brought from Hamlet to his mother, presumably telling her everything. Moreover, on the basis of Claudius' remark at the end of the churchyard scene:

Good Gertrude, set some watch upon your son,

we may imagine that mother and son have ample time to discuss the whole situation. However that may be, the Queen would be certain that Hamlet's life was in the greatest danger, and she would be watching Claudius' every move. It is very likely, to say the least, that she is suspicious of the drink that Claudius has prepared for her son, and that she drinks from it herself to test it. Though not clear from the text, this can be made clear by the actress. But even if we do not accept this interpretation, Shakespeare has completed his symbolism beyond all doubt by making her final words whole-heartedly on the side of her son:

No, no, the drink, the drink, – O my dear Hamlet, –
The drink, the drink! – I am poison'd.

As to Hamlet's last words, it is perhaps significant that they are a message to Fortinbras. This, together with the entry of Fortinbras immediately after Hamlet's death marks a certain continuity between the dead prince and the living one. There is a suggestion – nothing more – that Hamlet is mysteriously reborn in Fortinbras, though Shakespeare does not indicate this 'alchemy' explicitly here as he does in *Henry IV*. At the end of *Hamlet* the stress lies rather on the fruit of rebirth. 'Except a man be born again . . .' If the play as a whole corresponds to an interpenetration of Dante's *Inferno* and *Purgatorio*, the *Paradiso* is none the less not merely implicit. It is expressly anticipated in Horatio's farewell prayer for Hamlet:

Flights of angels sing thee to thy rest!

CHAPTER 5

OTHELLO

The essential feature of man's primordial state was the union of his soul with the Spirit; and one of the most universal symbols of the regaining of that state is marriage, the union of lovers. The prototype of this symbolism in Christianity lies in Christ's own references to himself as 'the Bridegroom'; and the Middle Ages were dominated by the conception of the Church or, microcosmically, the soul as the bride of Christ. Let us quote from the beginning of Ruysbroek's *The Adornment of the Spiritual Marriage*:

This Bridegroom is Christ, and human nature is the bride; the which God has made in His own image and after His likeness. And in the beginning He had set her in the highest and most beautiful, the richest and most fertile place in all the earth; that is, in Paradise. And He had given her dominion over all Creatures; and He had adorned her with graces; and had given her a commandment, so that by obedience she might have merited to be confirmed and established with her Bridegroom in an eternal troth, and never to fall into any grief, or any sin.

Then came a beguiler, the hellish fiend, full of envy, in the shape of a subtle serpent . . . And the fiend seduced the bride of God with false counsel; and she was driven into a strange country, poor and miserable and captive and oppressed, and beset by her enemies; so that it seemed as though she might never attain reconciliation and return again to her native land.

But when God thought the time had come, and had mercy on the suffering of His beloved, He sent His Only Begotten Son to earth, in a fair chamber, in a glorious temple; that is, in the body of the Virgin Mary. There he was married to his bride, our nature.[1]

[1] Translated by C. A. Wynschenk Dom.

Medieval art was continually expressing this union, in various ways, as for example in pictures of the mystical marriage of St Catharine of Alexandria with Christ, she representing the perfect soul and he the Spirit. But the Virgin Mary, in virtue of her Assumption and Coronation and her function as Co-Redemptress, also stands for the Spirit, and so by extension may a perfect woman. In *The Divine Comedy*, when Dante reaches the Garden of Eden on the top of the Mountain of Purgatory, Beatrice his beloved, personifying spiritual wisdom, descends from Heaven and the two meet in the terrestrial Paradise; and in *The Faerie Queene*, the sequel to the Red Crosse Knight's victory over the dragon is his marriage to the Lady Una.

In *Othello* the black Moor and his white lady are soul and Spirit. Like Cordelia, Desdemona is 'the pearl of great price' which was wantonly thrown away. Othello describes himself as:

> *One whose hand*
> *Like the base Judean threw a pearl away*
> *Richer than all his tribe.*

As for Iago, Othello says of him, after his iniquity has been revealed:

> *I look down towards his feet; but that's a fable,*

meaning: I look down to see the devil's cloven hooves; but since I see that Iago, who is unquestionably the devil, has ordinary human feet, I now learn that the current idea about the devil's feet is a mere fable. Then he strikes at Iago with his sword saying:

> *If that thou be'st a devil, I cannot kill thee*

and in fact he cannot kill him. Iago remarks to Lodovico:

> *I bleed, sir, but not killed.*

The sudden and secret marriage of Othello and Desdemona at the beginning of the play has taken Iago by surprise. But this union of soul and Spirit is only virtual; it marks the outset of the spiritual path, not the end, and symbolizes initiation rather than realization; and the first scene opens upon the devil preparing to do all in his power to wreck the marriage before it can come to fullness. To start with he can do little, for although husband and wife are temporarily separated, the Senate agrees that Desdemona shall follow Othello to Cyprus; but their first night there together is disturbed by the drunken brawl which Iago has staged; and the next morning he begins to imbue Othello with the suspicion that

Desdemona is unfaithful to him, so that the two lovers are never really in peace together until at the end they are lying dead side by side upon the marriage bed. Only then, after it has passed through the 'narrow gate' of death, is the soul truly united with the Spirit.

But it has a foretaste of Paradise, when the Moor arrives in Cyprus to find that Desdemona is already there before him. Her speedy coming has been almost miraculous, for as Cassio says:

> *Tempests themselves, high seas and howling winds,*
> *The gutter'd rocks, and congregated sands,*
> *Traitors ensteep'd to clog the guiltless keel,*
> *As having sense of beauty, do omit*
> *Their mortal natures, letting go safely by*
> *The divine Desdemona.*   (II, 1)

When Othello enters he says:

> *It gives me wonder great as my content*
> *To see you here before me. O my soul's joy!*
> *If after every tempest come such calms,*
> *Let the winds blow till they have waken'd death!*
> *And let the labouring bark climb hills of seas*
> *Olympus-high, and duck again as low*
> *As hell's from heaven!*

We have here an anticipation of the terrible 'storm' that is to follow, but also, in a sense, a guarantee of the final peace.

It may be asked: If Desdemona symbolizes the Spirit, why does she not see through Iago, as Cordelia would undoubtedly have done? But apart from the fact that Desdemona's proneness to think well of people unless given good reasons for not doing so is an aspect of her generosity and childlikeness and therefore part of her perfection, it must be remembered that a symbol can never account for every aspect of the higher reality that it symbolizes. One has the impression that no one was more critical of Shakespeare's symbols than the author himself and that he was continually striving to make them fuller and more all-embracing. It is probable that Claudius in *Hamlet* represents Shakespeare's own consciousness of the inadequacy of Falstaff as a personification of the devil; and Iago is certainly an 'improvement' on Claudius. Similarly the transcendence of Cordelia no doubt partly reflects Shakespeare's consciousness of certain shortcomings in Desdemona as a personification of the Spirit. None the less, granted that a symbol must always fall short in some respects, Desdemona is unquestionably adequate to fulfil her function in this play. She is convincingly perfect, and human perfection is a mirror for Divine Perfection. Moreover, she is the ideal complement to Othello. The ancient world and the Middle Ages held that every human being is perfectly matched by another human being of the opposite sex. The two may be separated by time and space and may never meet in this life, but if they do, no ordinary earthly passion can compare with the love that each feels for the other. Consequently, since a true symbol must be perfect of its kind, we may say that where the symbolism of sexual love is used, only such total and 'absolute' love as this is fully worthy to represent the primordial relationship between soul and Spirit, and it is clear that Shakespeare had no less than such love in mind when he drew the characters of Romeo and Juliet, for example, of Othello and Desdemona, and of Antony and Cleopatra. In *Othello*, as in these other plays, we are made to feel that there is something cosmic and universal in the intense mutual attraction between the lovers; and our thoughts leap to identify themselves with Othello's when he says in the last scene, with reference to his wife's death:

> *Methinks it should be now a huge eclipse*
> *Of sun and moon, and that the affrighted globe*
> *Should yawn at alteration.*

Iago, by far the most villainous of all Shakespeare's villains, is his last representation of the devil as such, and it is difficult to conceive how this representation could be surpassed. In his subsequent plays, as we shall see, it suits his purpose better to let his villains represent certain aspects of evil, without actually personifying evil's root. Edmund, in *King Lear*, is no doubt the second most villainous of Shakespeare's villains, but there is no common measure between him and Iago as regards what motivates their crimes. Edmund's chief motive is worldly ambition, whereas Iago's villainy is ultimately determined by love of evil and hatred of good. They have none the less much in common as regards outlook, and this outlook serves, incidentally, as a clear indication of where Shakespeare stands in the transition from Middle Ages to Renaissance which was still not quite complete in the England of his day. More than once his drama is a meeting place, almost a battleground, for the two points of view; and it is significant that Iago and Edmund are both out and out humanists, that is, typically representative of the Renaissance, and typical rebels against medieval tradition. Iago even goes so far as to deny the existence of virtue as an ideal since that implies, most unhumanistically, that there is some power above man which sets a standard for man to conform to.

> *Virtue! a fig! 'tis in ourselves that we are*
> *thus or thus. Our bodies are our gardens to the*
> *which our wills are gardeners . . . If the balance*
> *of our lives had not one scale of reason to poise*
> *another of sensuality, the blood and baseness of*
> *our natures would conduct us to most preposterous*
> *conclusions; but we have reason to cool our raging*
> *motions, our carnal stings, our unbitted lusts.* (I, 3)

Iago might almost have said: 'Thou, reason, art my goddess' just as Edmund does in fact say

> *Thou, nature, art my goddess.* (I, 2)

Either remark is centrally humanist, for according to humanism, humanity is the highest thing in existence, and humanity as such is limited to reason and to nature. Beyond reason, which marks nature's upper boundary, the supernatural begins. Under the flag of Renaissance humanism, naturalism in art and rationalism in thought march together side by side. It is clearly humanism, the rationalistic denial of all that is superhuman and supernatural that the medieval Hamlet means by the word 'philosophy' when he says:

> *There are more things in heaven and earth, Horatio,*
> *Than are dreamt of in your philosophy.*[2] (I, 5)

Nor can there be any doubt that Hamlet is here voicing Shakespeare's own view. The same may be said of the equally medieval Duke of Vienna in *Measure for Measure* when he sums up Barnardine's badness:

> *Sirrah, thou art said to have a stubborn soul*
> *That apprehends no further than this world.* (V, 1)

In *Othello*, unlike *Hamlet*, Hell and Purgatory are treated separately and successively. Almost the whole of *Othello* is taken up with the descent into Hell: the soul, personified by the Moor, gradually plumbs the very depths of error, that is, of thinking that black is white and white is black, that falsehood is truth and truth falsehood. But although the

---

[2] These lines are certainly not directed against Horatio. The possessive 'your' is here general and impersonal. The Arden editors quote as a parallel Hamlet's *Your worm is your only emperor for diet.*

descent is gradual, there is no correspondingly gradual development of soul in this play. The first stage of the journey only becomes spiritually effective when, at the bottom of Hell, the truth suddenly breaks in upon Othello like a flash of lightning which lights up in retrospect the whole descent that he had made in darkness, and he is transformed in an instant from a dupe to a wise man. Then follows Purgatory, with an equally concentrated brevity. Although compressed into only a few lines, its anguish is so intense that it altogether convinces us of expiation and purification. Othello anticipates, and therefore wears out to nothing, all that would have separated him from Desdemona, *this heavenly sight*, on the Day of Judgement, *when we shall meet at compt*. He cries out:

> *Whip me ye devils,*
> *From the possession of this heavenly sight!*
> *Blow me about in winds! roast me in sulphur!*
> *Wash me in steep-down gulfs of liquid fire!*   (v. 2)

Then, as it were in sign that his expiation is complete, a deep calm settles upon his sadness almost from that moment until the end.

The everlasting union of soul and Spirit after death is indicated by Othello's dying *upon a kiss* and also by the *marriage sheets* on the bed of death,[3] a detail that Shakespeare stresses just as much as he stresses the fact of Henry IV's death in the Jerusalem Chamber.

Everything is really explained in the Moor's own objective judgement of himself at the end when he tells the Venetians that they must speak of him as

> *Of one that loved not wisely but too well,*
> *Of one not easily jealous but being wrought*
> *Perplex'd in the extreme.*

He does not mean by the words *not wisely but too well* that he had loved Desdemona too much, but on the contrary that he had not loved her enough. Wisdom here is certainly not worldly wisdom such as might limit the extent of passion, but wisdom in the higher sense which would have added its light to the heat of passion and made him *see* that Desdemona was in fact goodness itself. Then he would have been proof

---

[3] Antony says in what is symbolically the same situation as Othello's:
> *I will be*
> *A bridegroom in my death, and run into't*
> *As to a lover's bed.*
> (IV, 14)

against Iago's deceptions, whereas a blind love which had too much passion in proportion to its wisdom made him a relatively easy victim. In this play it is blindness above all that characterizes fallen man, leaving a loophole for him to be *wrought*, that is, worked on by the devil, until he is so *perplexed* that he comes to believe the exact opposite of the truth.

Unlike Shakespeare's other heroes, the Moor is almost perfect even at the outset, and this partly helps to make the quickness of his passage through Purgatory so convincing. It is as if only one element were lacking to complete his perfection, an element of wisdom or vision. Now the descent into Hell for the discovery of the soul's worst possibilities is only necessary because these possibilities are an integral part of the psychic substance and need to be recovered, purified and reintegrated, for in order to be perfect the soul must be complete. This question will have to be considered more fully in connection with *Measure for Measure*. For the moment it is enough to bear in mind that the lost and perverted elements have first to be found and then redeemed, and that the interval between finding and redemption is likely to be fraught with danger. The case of Othello might be described by saying that when he reaches the bottom of Hell he finds a hitherto unknown blind eye, namely the lost element of vision, lying in the depths of his soul. *Corruptio optimi pessima*,[4] and since this eye, as well as being virtually the most precious, is also the most powerful of the psychic elements, it is able to transmit its blindness to the rest of the soul, and he throws away 'the pearl of great price'. Then dawns the truth. Shakespeare achieves here an overwhelming impact of a kind which drama alone, of all the arts, makes possible. Emilia's revelation of the innocence of Desdemona and the villainy of Iago, her instantaneous and dazzlingly clear proof that white is white and black is black, comes as a *fiat lux*, an irresistible Divine command: 'Let there be light'. The blind eye is filled with light and takes its rightful place at the summit of the soul. 'The stone which the builders rejected is become the head of the corner.'

---

[4] 'Corruption of the best is corruption at its worst.'

CHAPTER 6

MEASURE FOR MEASURE

It had become almost a 'tradition' until about twenty years ago that *Measure for Measure*, the 'bitter comedy', should leave an unpleasant taste in the mouth. It was liable to do so because a superficial first glance at the play is liable to set a director's imagination flowing in the wrong channels. It is immediately obvious which parts are dramatically the most effective, whence the temptation to subordinate everything to these two parts, as if the play were entitled *Angelo and Isabella* on the lines of Shakespeare's double-titled tragedies. If such an idea is allowed to govern the production, and if everything is done to make the audience feel that the essence of the play lies in the clash between these two characters, then the whole balance of one of Shakespeare's masterpieces will be in danger of being upset from the very start.

What is not obvious at first is the basic resemblance between *Measure for Measure* and two other plays which are practically never mentioned with it in the same breath, namely *A Midsummer Night's Dream* and *The Tempest*. It is true that as regards setting they are as remote from it as the supernatural is from the subnatural. What indeed could be more remote from an enchanted wood and an enchanted island than a corrupt city centred round its prison? But this difference is far outweighed by the fact that in all three plays the events can be viewed from a heavenly as well as from an earthly angle, and the audience are permitted to take the higher standpoint not merely at the end as in other Shakespearean plays, but also to a certain extent throughout. In *Measure for Measure* the skylight which makes this possible is the Duke of Vienna; and if it be admitted, as it readily will be, that no parts can be considered more important in *A Midsummer Night's Dream* and *The Tempest* than those of Oberon and Prospero, it must be admitted that the part of the Duke is equally important in the third play.

During the last few years more than one director has taken this into consideration, allowing the Duke to dominate the play as Shakespeare clearly intended that he should; and these productions have demonstrated that far from deserving the epithet 'bitter', *Measure for Measure* is penetrated by a deep serenity which makes it, despite its setting, a herald of the plays of the poet's final period.

Measure for Measure was written about the same time as *Hamlet* and *Othello*, either between the two[1] or shortly after them. In *Hamlet* and *Othello* the devil is represented by a separate character as if he were entirely outside the human soul whose spiritual journey is the deeper theme of the play. Such a manner of representation makes it possible to paint the devil in his true colours and to portray the hero in such a way as to give a definite foretaste of the perfection towards which he is being developed. But in actual fact the first part of the spiritual journey is chiefly concerned with the devil's inward presence, which can best be conveyed by foregoing any separate representation of him and by revealing diabolical elements in the soul of the hero; and if the dramatist sets out to do this, he immediately finds himself in something of a dilemma. If the diabolical is not painted sufficiently black, the meaning will be lost; but if it is painted black enough, there is a risk that the audience's sympathies will be alienated from the hero, and this will be fatal to the 'alchemy' of the play, for they will not be able to identify themselves with the Everyman that he represents.

In *Measure for Measure* Shakespeare ventures to represent the devil as being inside the soul and at the same time avoids spoiling the effect of his play through the device of portraying Everyman three times, in three closely inter-woven plots. These are, to name each after its central character, the plots of Isabella, Angelo, and Claudio. In the second of these Everyman has an unmistakably satanic devil inside him; but although we are in consequence alienated from Angelo, and although we are scarcely given time at the end to become fully reconciled to him – though it is up to a good actor to achieve a reconciliation with the

[1] But for this possible exception, the chapters are arranged according to the order in which the plays are generally agreed to have been written. For a more complete list of the later plays, *All's Well That Ends Well* and *Troilus and Cressida* must be added between *Hamlet* and *Othello*, and *Coriolanus*, *Timon of Athens* and *Pericles* between *Antony and Cleopatra* and *Cymbeline*.

audience – this does not spoil the effect of the play, because there are two other souls for us to identify ourselves with, while at the same time the three plots are so inextricable that the clearly established inwardness of the devil in one may serve, as it were by refraction, for his inwardness in the others.

Psychologically, the two characters Othello and Angelo are so different that they are scarcely ever thought of in the same context; but the two spiritual paths traced out by these two characters are 'rhythmically' almost identical. In both cases the slow descent into Hell, which takes up almost the whole play, teminates with a sudden dazzling flash of truth and is followed by a Purgatory which is compressed into only a few lines but which in each case is altogether convincing in virtue of its intensity.

One of the keys to understanding in general the descent into Hell, and in particular the part of Angelo as well as corresponding parts in other plays of Shakespeare, is Mariana's speech in the final scene:

> They say best men are moulded out of faults,
> And for the most become much more the better
> For being a little bad; so may my husband.

As we have seen in the case of Othello, the soul cannot be made perfect until it is complete. In order to reverse the process of the Fall by which part of man's soul came under the domination of the devil, it is necessary first of all to regain consciousness of the lost psychic elements which lie in dormant or semi-dormant perversion in the nethermost depths of the soul. Thus it is that in some traditional stories the descent into Hell is represented by a journey into the depths of the earth in search of hidden treasure: the lost psychic elements are symbolized by precious stones which have been stolen and hidden by diabolically cunning dwarfs. The second part of the spiritual path is concerned with the winning back of the lost jewels, that is, the freeing of the rediscovered psychic substance from the devil's domination;

If in *Othello* the fallenness of fallen man is represented as blindness, in *Measure for Measure* the stress is on incompleteness, at any rate as far as Angelo is concerned. At the beginning of the play Angelo appears to be by certain standards almost perfect, but as yet he is merely a human fragment. The Duke is well aware of this; he is also aware that beneath Angelo's limitations there lies a deep sincerity of purpose coupled with a sincere desire for perfection. Certainly, it is not from any intent to harm him but rather to help him to know himself that the Duke confers on him the vice-regency. It is this 'initiation' which marks for Angelo the beginning of the descent into the hidden depths of his own soul.

What is traditionally known as 'the descent into Hell' is termed so because through it the lower possibilities of the soul are revealed. But the modern development of psychoanalysis makes it necessary to explain that this first phase of the mystic path is radically different from any psychoanalytical descent into the subconscious. Psychoanalysis is largely a case of the blind leading the blind, for it is simply one soul working upon another without the help of any transcendent power. But initiation, followed up by the devotional and ascetic practices that are implicit in it, opens the door to contact with the perfecting and unifying power of the Spirit, whose presence demands that the psychic substance shall become once again a single whole. The more or less scattered elements of this substance are thus compelled to come together; and some of them come in anger, from dark and remote hiding-places, with the infernal powers still attached to them. From this point of view it is truer to say that Hell rises than that the mystic descends; and the result of this rising is a battle between the 'mighty opposites', with the soul as battleground. The mystic fights, by definition, on the side of Heaven; but the enemy will spare no stratagem to seduce him into fighting on the wrong side.

In no play does Shakespeare represent more clearly than in *Measure for Measure* the dangers of the spiritual path. At the outset of the path the perverted psychic elements are more or less dormant and remote from the centre of consciousness. They must first of all be woken and then redeemed, for they cannot be purified in their sleep; and it is when they wake in a state of raging perversion that there is always the risk that they will overpower the whole soul. This is what happens with Angelo; but in his case it is necessary that he should be overcome for a while by his lower self in order that his pride may be broken; and in the end he is saved by his basic sincerity which calls down a Divine Grace personified by the Duke.

The chaos in Angelo's soul is instantly reduced to order in the final scene by the flash of truth which is brought about by the sudden appearance of the Duke from beneath his disguise as the Friar. Then begins Purgatory, and Angelo dies as it were ten thousand deaths in the space of a few minutes. But by the beginning of the last scene, even before the appearance of the Duke, Angelo was no longer merely a human fragment: his soul was a chaos of warring virtue and vice, with vice momentarily in the ascendant, but it was at least a complete soul;

and it is because the fallen soul in quest of perfection has first of all to be made complete by the addition of faults, which are only subsequently purified and transformed into virtues, that Mariana says:

> They say best men are moulded out of faults.

In Shakespeare's maturer plays there are many echoes of his earlier plays, sometimes as if the author felt that he had failed to do justice to a good idea, and wished to try his hand again. There can be little doubt that *The Taming of the Shrew* was in his mind when he conceived the central theme of *Measure for Measure*, but his treatment of the Duke and Isabella is as subtle as his treatment of Petruchio and Katharina is crude. Perhaps if he could have foreseen the fate of *Measure for Measure* in the hands of posterity, he would have made the 'taming' of Isabella a little less subtle, or at any rate made his intention more explicitly unmistakeable. But we must remember that he wrote on the understanding that he would produce his own plays, or at least be present at the production.

Whenever Isabella jars on us, she was certainly intended to jar. At the beginning of the play she appears, like Angelo, to have a certain perfection, but like him she is no more than a human fragment. Nor could she ever have become fully herself by following the spiritual path that she has already chosen. On the contrary, one feels that the very sacrifices she plans to make would have merely increased the one-sidedness of her development. It is significant that the first words we hear her speak are an expression of disappointment that the nuns of St Clare – one of whom she hopes to become – are not bound by stricter rules. She is prepared to throw herself wholeheartedly into a life of celibacy, fasting and prayer; but Providence refuses the sacrifices she is prepared to make which would no doubt have been relatively easy for her and demands in their place sacrifices of an altogether different nature. Isabella's shortcoming which she has to make good is shown up very clearly in the prison scene when her brother asks her to save his life at the price of her chastity. Shakespeare clearly intends us to think that she is right in refusing; but he does not intend us to think that she is right in saying to her brother:

> Die, perish! Might but my bending down
> Reprieve thee from thy fate, it should proceed,
> I'll pray a thousand prayers for thy death,
> No word to save thee.

We know that the Duke is listening to this speech; and though he never comments on the hard and self-righteous streak in Isabella's character, what he arranges for her to do in the last act of the play is such a perfect 'measure for measure' that there can be no doubt that it is based on a full knowledge of her particular fault. For first of all she is called upon to make a false declaration in public that she did sacrifice her chastity; and secondly she is called upon to go on her knees and beg for the life of the man who, as she believes, has most terribly wronged both her and her brother, and on whom, with her all too human sense of justice, she is thirsting to have her revenge. Let us recall the situation. Mariana goes on her knees to beg pardon for Angelo. Isabella stands in silence beside her. The Duke refuses Mariana's request; again she asks, and again he refuses. We must imagine that he is longing for Isabella to intervene, but the intervention must come unprompted by him. She still stands there in silence. Then Mariana turns to Isabella and says:

> Sweet Isabel, take my part;
> Lend me your knees, and, all my life to come,
> I'll lend you all my life to do you service.

Isabella makes no movement, and the Duke says:

> Against all sense you do importune her:
> Should she kneel down in mercy of this fact,
> Her brother's ghost his paved bed would break,
> And take her hence in horror.

Mariana is not to be silenced, but continues:

> Isabel,
> Sweet Isabel, do yet but kneel by me:

Isabella still stands like a figure of stone:

> Hold up your hands, say nothing, I'll speak all,

says Mariana, but Isabella's hands remain at her sides. Mariana goes on:

> They say best men are moulded out of faults,
> And, for the most, become much more the better
> For being a little bad; so may my husband.
> O, Isabel! will you not lend a knee?

> He dies for Claudio's death,

says the Duke. Then at last Isabella steps forward and goes on her knees beside Mariana. The Duke has created this situation, deliberately makings things as difficult as possible for her, so that her intervention when it finally comes, may be a real triumph over herself. The victory which is symbolized in *Hamlet* by revenge is symbolized in *Measure for Measure* by the foregoing of revenge.

The part of Claudio runs parallel to those of Angelo and Isabella. For him the most difficult thing in the world is to become resigned to the idea of death. The Duke, although determined to prevent his execution, holds out no hope of life to him until he has attained and made firm the necessary resignation. When Claudio says to him:

> *I have hope to live and am prepared to die,*

he replies:

> *Be absolute for death; either death or life*
> *Shall thereby be the sweeter.*

At the end of the Duke's speech, Claudio says:

> *I humbly thank you.*
> *To sue to live, I find I seek to die,*
> *And, seeking death, find life: let it come on.*

Later, however, he becomes unsettled again, and the Duke says to him:

> *prepare yourself to death.*
> *Do not satisfy your resolution with hopes that*
> *are fallible: tomorrow you must die; go to*
> *your knees and make ready;*

and when Claudio replies that he is *out of love with life*, the Duke insists: *Hold you there!*

This third theme of the play, far simpler yet no less profound than the other two, sums up the spiritual path as a 'dying into life'.

Outwardly *Measure for Measure* represents, in Shakespeare's art, a more direct continuity with the Middle Ages than is to be found in any of his other plays. Consequently, it is not too much to assume that to its earliest audiences, who still had much of the Middle Ages in them, this play would have presented no problems. They would not, for example, with a purely psychological interpretation, have pitied Mariana for being married to such a man as Angelo, for they would have sensed that by the end Angelo had been washed as white as snow. Nor would they have disliked Isabella for taking so long to be merciful, for they would have realized that at the moment of her going down on her knees, the last flaw in an otherwise perfect soul had been forever effaced.

It is by no means impossible to make this clear to a modern audience also; but to no audience can the play be wholly acceptable unless they are made to feel, as unremittingly as possible, that all spiritual wisdom is embodied in the Duke, who personifies the transcendence of the claims of the next world over this world and whose presence in this world is, to use Angelo's words, *like power Divine*.[2] The Duke is trebly a symbol of the Spirit. Firstly, he is the spiritual guide of the three souls in quest of perfection. Secondly, Isabella's marriage with him at the end means no less than the perfected soul's union with the Spirit; for everybody in a sense, but for her in particular, the beginning of the last scene recalls the words of the Gospel; 'Behold, the Bridegroom cometh, go ye out to meet him.' It is in virtue of being in a sense a prolongation of the Duke that the faithful Mariana may be said to stand for the Spirit[3] in relation to Angelo, to whom the Duke says:

> *Love her, Angelo!*
> *I have confess'd her and I know her virtue.*   (V, 1)

Thirdly, when the Duke takes his seat on the throne to pronounce the final verdicts, there is an unmistakable impression – certainly intended by Shakespeare – of the Last Judgement, an impression which is made all the stronger because although, literally speaking, the Duke was merely disguised as a priest, we have none the less come to look on him as an incarnation of the two functions of spiritual authority and temporal power merged into one. Moreover we cannot help noticing, in retrospect, another resemblance between him and Doomsday's Judge: although supposed to be 'absent', he has in fact been present all the time.

---

[2] This has been well brought out in some recent productions.

[3] There is nothing transcendent about Juliet, whom Claudio marries. But there is no need to analyze this last marriage, since it may be said to bask in the sun of the other two marriages and to borrow its symbolism from theirs.

CHAPTER 7

MACBETH

Macbeth is the only play of Shakespeare's in which the powers of darkness are shown on the stage, distinct and separate from the human characters. Of the three levels in the hierarchy of the universe, the subhuman witches personify Hell, and they have been drawn up to the human plane by the evil in Macbeth's soul. It is made abundantly clear in the scene of their first encounter with him that before they sought him out he had already formed the intention to kill the King; and it becomes evident from a later scene that he and his wife had already plotted the murder together.

Nor is it only the lowest level of existence that is particularly clear cut in this play. Without introducing any divine characters as he does into his last plays, Shakespeare is none the less at pains to counterbalance the powers of darkness by sharply defined 'powers of light'. In *Hamlet*, as we have seen, the murdered king has a double aspect like Adam himself, one fallen and the other unfallen. But in *Macbeth* Duncan represents nothing if not sanctity. Too little care is taken in many productions to ensure that the representatives of Heaven are sufficiently impressive. The short but beautifully written part of Duncan calls for an actor who will, from the start, make convincing what Macduff says of him to Malcolm towards the end of the play:

> *Thy royal father*
> *Was a most sainted king* (IV, 3)

The same applies no less urgently to the actor who plays Malcolm, the prolongation of Duncan.

There can be little doubt that the totally unnecessary Act I scene 2 –
badly written from more than one angle – is a later interpolation, not by
Shakespeare. The omission of this scene makes our first sight of the King
all the more royal for being in the Palace of Fores. Duncan is an elderly
man, of whom it can be said, as we are clearly intended to think, that he
has 'one foot already in Paradise'; and having confronted us with this
personification of the highest of the three levels of possibility for man,
Shakespeare loses no time in setting before us the intermediary degree,
that of Purgatory, which is implicit in the description of the death of the
former Thane of Cawdor who has just been executed for treason, the
very sin which, as we know, is being hatched in the soul of the new
Thane of Cawdor, Macbeth. It is Malcolm who speaks:

> *I have spoke*
> *With one who saw him die: who did report*
> *That very frankly he confess'd his treasons,*
> *Implor'd your highness' pardon, and set forth*
> *A deep repentance. Nothing in his life*
> *Became him like the leaving it . . .*

> *There's no art* [says Duncan]
> *To find the mind's construction in the face:*
> *He was a gentleman on whom I built*
> *An absolute trust*   (I, 4)

The equally inscrutable, equally trusted and even more treacherous
Macbeth enters at this moment – generally recognized as one of the
greatest moments of irony in all drama; and it is soon followed by
another comparable moment when the King announces his intention of
spending the night at Macbeth's castle and when his host-to-be takes
leave to go ahead of him to see that due preparations are made:

> *I'll be myself the harbinger, and make joyful*
> *The hearing of my wife with your approach.*

Duncan has just proclaimed:

> *Sons, kinsmen, thanes,*
> *And you whose places are the nearest, know*
> *We will establish our estate upon*
> *Our eldest, Malcolm whom we name hereafter*
> *The Prince of Cumberland: which honour must*
> *Not, unaccompanied, invest him only,*
> *But signs of nobleness, like stars, shall shine*
> *On all deservers.*

It is significant that he should express himself in terms of light. Macbeth is no doubt meant here as the chief of those on whom secondary honours *like stars shall shine*. If he had been made Prince of Cumberland,[1] this might have deflected him from his criminal purpose; but the investiture of a much younger man precipitates the irrevocable crystallization of his worst intent. Lucifer-like, he disdains being the brightest of secondary brilliances. In his aside to the audience as he leaves the stage, his words *Stars, hide your fires* have thus a double sense, for they take up the words of the King, and are a proud rejection of all the secondary honours,[2] as well as marking the choice of darkness in preference to light. The aside as a whole is:

> *The Prince of Cumberland! – That is a step*
> *On which I must fall down, or else o'erleap,*
> *For in my way it lies. Stars, hide your fires!*
> *Let not light see my black and deep desires;*
> *The eye wink at the hand; yet let that be,*
> *Which the eye fears, when it is done, to see.*

The eye is here the light of the conscience; Macbeth's wilful suppression of that light is paralleled in the next scene by Lady Macbeth:

> *Come, thick night,*
> *And pall thee in the dunnest smoke of hell,*
> *That my keen knife see not the wound it makes,*
> *Nor heaven peep through the blanket of the dark,*
> *To cry, 'Hold, hold!'*

Both protagonists resolve to be deaf henceforth to all promptings of their better natures, and Lady Macbeth keeps to this implacably until she finally breaks, towards the end of the play, beneath the strain of the murder's terrible aftermath which she had refused to foresee. The further-sighted Macbeth, who does not break, also differs from his wife in having certain initial hesitations. At one point he even decides to forego the murder or at least to postpone it; but the reason he gives when he announces his decision amounts to nothing more creditable than the reaction of one kind of egoism against another:

---

[1] As a near kinsman, he could have hoped for this. The throne of Scotland was not then strictly hereditary; Prince of Cumberland was the title of the heir designate.

[2] Later he goes back on this attitude, but only for a brief moment.

> *We will proceed no further in this business:*
> *He hath honoured me of late; and I have bought*
> *Golden opinions from all sorts of people*
> *Which would be worn now in their newest gloss,*
> *Not cast aside so soon.*   (1.7)

Most of the other reasons given are equally untranscendent, such as the fear of suffering retribution in this life – he says explicitly that he is prepared to *jump*[3] *the life to come* – and the fear that they may fail in their attempt; and the ease with which Lady Macbeth wins him back to his criminal intention betrays the extreme superficiality of the few moral scruples that he has left. These scruples, the faint residue of light which still remains in his soul, are reflected in the following arguments which he adds to those we have just given. In themselves they are good, but they serve to eliminate all possibility of excuse, for once the murder has been committed they reveal in retrospect the cold-blooded deliberation of Macbeth's choice of evil:

> *He's here in double trust:*
> *First, as I am his kinsman and his subject,*
> *Strong both against the deed; then as his host,*
> *Who should against his murderer shut the door,*
> *Not bear the knife myself. Besides, this Duncan*
> *Hath borne his faculties*[4] *so meek, hath been*
> *So clear*[5] *in his great office, that his virtues*
> *Will plead like angels, trumpet-tongued, against*
> *The deep damnation of his taking off.*[6]   (1, 7)

The cause of the Fall of man is traditionally represented as the choice of a forbidden thing loved for its own sake in preference to the whole treasury of Paradisal blessings which are loveable above all for the sake of God whose presence they manifest. We have already seen from *Hamlet*[7] that this choice constitutes a murder. Primordial man was possessed of two natures; and it is not possible for man to choose evil rather than good unless his human nature discards his spiritual nature. Otherwise expressed, his lower nature has to do away with his higher nature. Throughout the first act of *Macbeth* the protagonists are literally

---

[3] Risk.
[4] Prerogatives of kingship.
[5] Innocent, spotless.
[6] Against the deeply damnable act of killing him.
[7] See p. .

preoccupied with the stifling of their better selves; and as a parallel to this psychological process by which they re-enact the Fall, it is the victim of their intended outward crime who symbolizes the higher nature they are seeking to eliminate. This symbolism is, moreover, subtly implicit in the above quoted passage, for each of man's two natures is *kinsman* to the other, and the lower is *subject* to the higher in addition to being its *host*. The Spirit can never be at home on earth, and insofar as it is present, it is always the guest of the soul.

What has been said so far amounts to saying that the audience can identify themselves with neither of the chief characters. In this respect *Macbeth* differs from all the plays we have so far considered as well as those which are the themes of the chapters to come. The presence of an Everyman on the stage serves to draw the audience into the drama. His absence makes it all the more imperative that they should be assimilated by other means; and the result of this challenge is a masterpiece in which Shakespeare the playwright achieves an unsurpassable intensity of dramatic dialogue and dramatic situation, while Shakespeare the poet amazes us with an art which he equals elsewhere but never excels.

To affirm that *Macbeth* is a superbly poetic morality play on the theme of ambition, deadly sin, worldly ruin, death and damnation is to speak the truth, but it is at the same time a simplification and an understatement. In scene after scene a perfection of writing is reached which makes the term 'fiction' totally inadequate. To say what one is tempted to say, that it is 'more real than life', might seem to be a pointless contradiction in terms. We will none the less go so far as to claim that it reveals something of the basic skeleton of reality which 'ordinary life' tends to hide; and in so doing it opens up a magnitude of vista which transcends the plane of morality. Or it could simply be said that *Macbeth* is the fruit of manifest inspiration, and that the presence of the Spirit will not be confined within the narrowness of a purely exoteric outlook, and that it refuses to be deprived of the mystical dimension of height and of depth which is its element.

Let us consider a significant section of the drama, beginning with Macbeth's words to his servant just before the dagger soliloquy which immediately precedes the murder:

> Go bid thy mistress, when my drink is ready,
> She strike upon the bell. Get thee to bed. (II, 1)

He knows that his wife will understand what he means, namely that the bell is to be the signal that everything is ready for the murder. When it rings, he says:

> *I go, and it is done: the bell invites me.*
> *Hear it not, Duncan; for it is a knell*
> *That summons thee to heaven, or to hell.*   (II, 1)

These words are a powerful reminder, preceded by other reminders, that this world is suspended between Heaven and Hell. But the mention of Hell does not concern Duncan, as Macbeth well knows, for he has already told us that Duncan is so excellent a man

> *that his virtues*
> *Will plead like angels, trumpet-tongued, against*
> *The deep damnation of his taking-off.*

We must not, however, suppose that it is merely the word 'knell' in the preceding line which compels the speaker to add the words *or to hell*. The compulsion of the rhyme is powerfully symbolic. It is not for Macbeth to be speaking of Heaven, for its gates are closed to him. He is compelled to complete the rhyme for exactly the same reason which prevents him, a few moments later, from saying 'Amen' when he hears one of the King's guards say *God bless us* and the other *Amen*:

> *But wherefore could I not pronounce 'Amen'?*
> *I had most need of blessing, and 'Amen'*
> *Stuck in my throat.*   (II, 2)

Macbeth utters the words *or to hell* with reference to himself. An actor could make this clear. It is, moreover, significant that the bell purports to be the signal that Macbeth's *drink is ready*, for this cannot be disconnected from something he has previously said, in another of his arguments against the murder:

> *This even-handed justice*
> *Commends the ingredients of our poisoned chalice*
> *To our own lips.*   (I, 7)

By *even-handed justice* he means the unbiassed law of actions followed by reactions which operates in this world. He tells himself that his own killing of Duncan would inevitably mean someone else's killing of him. To use his actual metaphor, Duncan's draught of death is Macbeth's draught of death. It is therefore yet another grim piece of irony – the play is full of them – that the bell which is in fact the signal that Duncan's 'drink' is ready should be given out by Macbeth as being the signal that his own drink is ready; and it is the double nature of the drink that makes the bell a double summons, *to heaven, or to hell* – to Heaven for Duncan, and to Hell for Macbeth.

The bell's fatal significance for Macbeth is also subtly confirmed by its juxtaposition with another stage effect of sound – one of the most powerful in all drama. After the servant has been sent to bed, the first uninhibited sound in the dark silence of the night is the bell, for soliloquys are thoughts not sounds, and the thought in question is largely concerned with silence:

> *Thou sure and firm-set earth,*
> *Hear not my steps, which way they walk, for fear*
> *Thy very stones prate of my whereabout*   (II, 1)

After the bell, apart from whatever undercurrent there may be from wind and owl and other voices of nature, there is again the silence of soliloquy or the half silence of the hushed dialogue between the murderer and his accomplice. The next full sound which follows that of the bell is the sudden knocking on the gate at the castle's south entry, a sound inexorably uninhibited and, unlike the bell, totally beyond the control of Macbeth and his wife. It is the signal, but this time in fact, not merely in pretence, that Macbeth's 'drink' is ready, or virtually so; for the knocker is Macduff, the man not *of woman born*, who is destined to administer the draught of death to Macbeth. But although the knocking – relentlessly louder and louder – is beyond Macbeth's control, he himself is none the less in one sense the knocker, for he has brought his doom upon his own head. The knocking is his, and the gate he knocks on is the gate of Hell, as we learn from the Porter.

As far as known crimes are concerned, it would seem that the bottom of Hell is reached with the murder of Lady Macduff and her children. This scene is immediately followed by the scene in England where Malcolm enlarges Everyman's vision of Hell, even beyond the guilt of Macbeth, by imputing all possible sins to himself. Once this point has been reached, there takes place a kind of purification where Malcolm solemnly disowns all the iniquities he has laid upon himself. It is also significant that true repentance is the theme of Malcolm's already quoted first speech in the play, when he tells his father, with regard to the treacherous Thane of Cawdor,

> *That very frankly he confessed his treasons,*
> *Implored your highness' pardon, and set forth*
> *A deep repentance . . .*

These indications would be too slight in themselves to warrant the claim that there is in *Macbeth* a substantial layer of meaning which corresponds to the second part of Dante's epic. The account of the repentance of the Thane of Cawdor does, however, serve to make the audience's thoughts dwell for a moment on the idea of atonement, and that is important, for it is from the auditorium that this play needs to borrow its purgatorial pilgrim. The above speech also serves to set up a standard of measurement from which it can be seen, by stark contrast, that the bitter regrets of the protagonists, however intense they may be, are very remote from *deep repentance*, without which there can be no question of Purgatory.

A distinction is to be made between the deliberate descent into Hell with a view to Purgatory, and the doomed descent of the damned. It is to these alone that the closing words of the inscription on Dante's gate applies:

Lasciate ogni speranza, voi ch'entrate.[8]

The terrible truth of these words is enacted in this tragedy. From the first knock onward, the scenes which concern Macbeth and his wife are like the *Inferno* without Dante himself. He, the author-spectator, who is privileged to enter Hell and then to leave it for Purgatory, corresponds to our play's spectator, who is invited – or compelled as the case may be – to build his own Purgatory on the basis of the two protagonists' Hell.

The audience can identify themselves, not with the actual crimes that Macbeth perpetrates, but with his sense of guilt, for it must be remembered that Christendom is by very definition a world of sinners acutely aware of standing in need of a Redeemer, a world avowedly steeped in such guilt as can only be outweighed by the Passion of the Divine Saviour. Moreover, the horror of the actual deed of murder suddenly and briefly restores to Macbeth something of his better nature. He is never so sympathetic throughout the play as he is at this moment of uncontrolled self-abhorrence. It does not last, being no more than a drawn out lightning flash in a pitch dark night, but it is long enough for the audience to identify themselves whole-heartedly with his sense of guilt, and to drink it into their souls. The intensity of his feeling thus enriches their own consciousness of sin and neediness. But they come together only to separate almost at once, for Macbeth's situation is so unbearable that they are impelled to dissociate themselves from it

---

[8] Give up every hope, ye who enter.

through the only possible outlet, which he is unable to take. However, fierce his regrets, he cannot repent, whereas they can; and that 'can' has now become, thanks to these moments of anguish, an imperative 'must'. They part company, he for the path of despair, and they for the path of atonement. By this means the dimension of Purgatory is surreptitiously added to the play.

There is also a second guilt in the state of original sin. The choice which caused the Fall was only possible because the soul had deliberately violated, and thereby partially paralyzed, its own sense of proportion; and by reason of this paralysis, fallen man tends to turn a blind eye to the enormity of his betrayal. In the first half of the play it is the temptress herself who voices this wilful blindness. The consciousness of sin is thus galvanized into life, for the best of the audience, not only by Macbeth's positive example but also, negatively, by the appalling example of its opposite in Lady Macbeth. A supreme instance is when she says, just after the murder:

A little water clears us of this deed.

As the pendulum of dialogue swings between husband and wife, the audience are 'accused' now of one guilt, now of the other, the guilt of sin and the guilt of 'innocence'; and in the murder scene they undergo this double onslaught to the accompaniment of the knocking, which sounds, as we have seen, the alarum of retribution and of doom.

It may be argued that these considerations no longer hold good, seeing that many members of a modern audience refuse to accept the notion of original sin and are not conscious of being fallen men. Perhaps the best answer to this would be the question: 'Are they not *sub*conscious of being fallen men?' However that may be, sacred art, to be operative, presupposes the full concept of human perfection, that is, the concept of sanctity, and thereby the awareness of falling short of that ideal. This awareness may be acknowledged by many of those who disown, by automatic modernist reaction, the term 'original sin'. Yet the imperfection in question is one and the same.

Shakespeare achieves his effect by what must be amongst the most powerful expressions of guilt in all literature. Their power lies not only in their poetry but also in their relevance, each to its moment in the drama. There is never any slackening of dramatic tension. The following extract may serve to recall the perfection of the whole.

As Lady Macbeth goes out with the daggers which Macbeth has forgotten to leave beside the sleeping guards, the silence is suddenly broken by the first knocking upon the gate. Macbeth is instantly shattered in soul:

> *Whence is that knocking?*
> *How is't with me, when every noise appals me?*

We may assume that he lifts his hand to clutch his head and sees again that they are covered with blood.

> *What hands are here? Ha! they pluck out mine eyes.*
> *Will all great Neptune's ocean wash this blood*
> *Clean from my hand? No, this my hand will rather*
> *The multitudinous seas incarnadine,*[9]
> *Making the green one red.*

Lady Macbeth now re-enters, calm and self-controlled[10] as before. At the next knocking she says:

> *I hear a knocking*
> *At the south entry: – retire we to our chamber.*
> *A little water clears us of this deed:*
> *How easy is it then!*

Macbeth's main answer to this comes at the sound of more knocking:

> *Wake Duncan with thy knocking: I would thou couldst!*   (II, 2)

He had said at the sound of the bell, the signal for the murder:

> *Hear it not, Duncan . . .*

Altogether overwhelmed, Everyman the spectator flees from damnation; and to further his escape, the knocking is there to lend his flight the wings of panic. In souls that are penetrated by the words of the liturgy, *qui tollis peccata mundi, O Thou that takest away the sins of the world,* an answer, or a solution, is bound to be generated, in varying degrees of consciousness, by Macbeth's question:

---

[9] Macbeth's anguish is so intense that ordinary language will not suffice to express it. This sudden spontaneous coining of two new words which strike us at once as marvellously right – nothing else will do – bear witness to the high degree of Shakespeare's inspiration.

[10] She too, however, had shuddered despite herself at what she had just seen, as we learn somewhat later from the cry she utters in her sleep:
> *Yet who would have thought the old man*
> *to have had so much blood in him!* (V, 1)

Will all great Neptune's ocean wash this blood
Clean from my hand?

The same could be said of Lady Macbeth's sleep-walking utterance:

Here's the smell of the blood still: all
the perfumes of Arabia will not sweeten
this little hand. (v, 1)

and of Macbeth's interrogation of her doctor:

Canst thou not minister to a mind diseased,
Pluck from the memory a rooted sorrow,
Raze out the written troubles of the brain,
And with some sweet oblivious antidote
Cleanse the stuff'd bosom of that perilous stuff
Which weighs upon the heart? (v, 3)

With regard to all such questions throughout the play, there is an implicit answer: 'No, but something else can', and in that answer there dawns a Purgatory within the murk of Hell. It is beside the point that some members of a modern audience are inclined to agree with Macbeth that:

Life's but a walking shadow; a poor player,
That struts and frets his hour upon the stage,
And then is heard no more: it is a tale
Told by an idiot, full of sound and fury,
Signifying nothing. (v, 5)

In the England of Shakespeare, such lines would have evoked, in addition to wonder at their beauty, a certain objective pity for the speaker but not a subjective assent. In other words, this speech would be taken as something parallel to the already quoted close of Dante's inscription on the gate of Hell:

Lasciate ogni speranza, voi ch'entrate

As to the dimension of Paradise in *Macbeth*, it must be added to what has already been said, that Malcolm, the man who, in life, was to be the husband of St Margaret, is clearly intended by Shakespeare to represent the ideal of kingship. To repeat an already made quotation with more of its context:

Thy royal father
Was a most sainted king: the queen that bore thee,
Oftener upon her knees than on her feet,
Died every day she lived.

Moreover, Malcolm is not only the true heir of both his parents; he is
also a prolongation of St Edward, the holy King of England who has
given him shelter and who helps him, by force of arms, to regain his
rightful heritage from the usurper tyrant. Malcolm's lines in praise of his
host are in no sense a digression. Many editors hasten to remark that this
speech (IV, 3) must have been written in compliment to King James: but
however that may be, it serves to strengthten in advance the effect of the
final scene by adding the authority of a known saint and king to that of
the relatively unknown Malcolm, who thus becomes still more qualified
to personify the ultimate triumph of good over evil.

This leads us to the consideration of a further significance in
Shakespeare's plays, a meaning which has been already mentioned but
not yet enlarged upon, although we are conscious of it in *Hamlet* and
Measure for Measure, as well as in *King Lear* and other later plays. We may
call it macrocosmic, for it corresponds to the significance of a cathedral
not as an image of the human being but as an image of the whole world.

This meaning has more prominence in *Macbeth* than in several of the
other great plays, but some may say that like the dogma of original sin
it is no longer accessible to most members of a modern audience,
because it runs directly counter to their evolutionism and their
progressism. It has indeed to be admitted that the two persuasions in
question still continue to linger on in many Western minds, considerably
affecting the general outlook, despite the facts, firstly that this century is
in itself so powerfully suggestive of the opposite of progress, and
secondly that in its latter half an increasing number of scientists have
written devastating refutations[11] of the theory of evolution on purely
scientific grounds. But the truth has its rights, and error's scope of
influence is limited, for human knowledge has two aspects, mental and
existential, which are respectively outward and inward, and it is only the
mind which is subject to error. In other words, man was created both to
think truth and to live truth; and though he may come to think error, he
does not live error. However much a person may have been

---

[11] See, for example, Douglas Dewar, *The Transformist Illusion*; Evan Shute, *Flaws in the
Theory of Evolution*.

indoctrinated, from childhood onwards, with the theory of evolution, its opposite, the truth of the Fall of man, remains indelibly written in the inner substance of the soul. Consequently, no one can be totally evolutionist: at the most, even today, it is a question of being divided against oneself. But normally the mind also is proof against error: evolutionism and progressism only became possible after religious faiths had weakened beyond a certain degree, and that degree had not nearly been reached by the end of the sixteenth century. In the world of Shakespeare – 'the world of Plato and St Augustine' – spiritual logic made it inconceivable that primordial man should not have been perfect. So long as men retained 'a sense of God', which is very different from a vague, unintelligent and therefore precarious piety, they knew that this earthly state – especially as regards mankind, its central feature – must have been at its unsurpassable best when it came from the hand of the Creator. The Book of Genesis and the Graeco-Roman doctrine of the Golden, Silver, Bronze and Iron Ages served to fill in certain details of a general conception of the rhythms of time[12] which was already inescapably implicit in the very nature of things, that is, in man as the image of God and, more generally, in earthly things as the shadows of spiritual realities. Beginning with primordial perfection, history was conceived as a record of the repeated backslidings of mankind which at a certain point were always suddenly checked by Divine Intervention – a retribution followed by a restoration of order. Moreover, Shakespeare and his contemporaries naturally expected the rhythm of the past to continue in the future. It still seemed to almost everyone, as it had done throughout the Middle Ages, that things were too bad for the second coming of Christ to be very far off. The words *Something is rotten in the state of Denmark* would have found an echo in every heart. But in any case, when they said: 'Thy kingdom come on earth!' they did not look for a gradual upward movement. If the sudden retribution were not immediately at hand, if the worst had not yet happened and if so-and-so were not the Antichrist, then things would have to go on growing worse and worse, as had been predicted, until finally they did reach their lowest point with the real Antichrist. Then, suddenly, the true Christ would come, the guilty would be destroyed and the remaining few would live on into the Millenium.

They saw how the world goes: a state of harmony, a fatal step of error

---

[12] For a fuller treatment of this question, see my *Ancient Beliefs and Modern Superstitions*, Ch. II (Allen and Unwin, Mandala Books, 1980).

or sin, growing discord, the passage from bad to worse, more or less sudden retribution, and restoration of harmony. This was the rhythm that they had seen in the miracle plays and that they now saw in *Hamlet* and *King Lear* – to name only two of those mirrors which Shakespeare holds up to the great cycle of time. The cosmic rhythm of *King Lear* is explicitly affirmed when Kent cries out at the terrible events in the last scene:

> *Is this the promis'd end?*

And Gloster had already said, with reference to the aged and demented king:

> *O ruin'd piece of nature! This great world*
> *Shall so wear out to naught.*   (IV, 6)

Macbeth is no anomaly as regards its macrocosmic significance. The plot in its main outlines is very similar to the plot of *Hamlet*. A good king is secretly murdered by a kinsman; the murderer succeeds in making himself king; he plunges further and further into guilt; things grow worse and worse; and finally the usurper is killed and the country enters upon another state of harmony under a new king.

In *Macbeth* the reign of King Duncan, like the reign of King Hamlet, corresponds to the Golden Age. The reign of Malcolm, like the reign of Fortinbras, corresponds to the Millennium.

CHAPTER 8

KING LEAR

King Lear has much in common with both *Hamlet* and *Othello*. As regards this last play, it is true that in *King Lear* the love theme concerns parent and child, whereas in *Othello* it concerns husband and wife; but the symbolism is unaffected by the difference. Lear and the Moor represent 'Everyman', the human soul, and Cordelia and Desdemona represent the Spirit. In both plays 'the pearl of great price' is thrown away; and in *King Lear* this is echoed in the sub-plot by Gloster's throwing away' of Edgar.

From a macrocosmic point of view, that is, considering the play is an image of the history of mankind, Lear's throwing away 'the pearl' represents the Fall. He is not banished from Paradise, which in this play is symbolized by the presence of Cordelia, but he himself banishes Paradise, which amounts to the same. Britain is no longer man's home but his exile. As Kent says:

> *Freedom lies hence and banishment is here.*   (I, 1)

And this inversion of the natural order of things is repeatedly indicated in various ways during the first scenes of the play, as when Kent exclaims ironically:

> *Kill thy physician and the fee bestow*
> *Upon the foul disease!*   (*ibid.*)

or when the Fool says:

> *Truth's a dog must to kennel; he must*
> *be whipped out when Lady the brach may stand*
> *by the fire and stink.*   (I, 4)

It is significant that Cordelia is Lear's third daughter. Like the apex of a triangle, the celestial number three symbolizes the resolution of oppositions (these being represented geometrically by the two lower corners of the triangle) into a transcendent harmony. Lear has banished harmony and left his kingdom at the mercy of discord, represented by Goneril and Regan. By exchanging three for two he has exchanged spiritual wisdom for worldly wisdom, that is, the dual wisdom of the Tree of the Knowledge of Good and Evil. The order of the day is henceforth worldly wisdom. The banishment of Cordelia is inevitably and quickly followed up by the banishment of Kent and Edgar. Of those characters who may be considered as prolongations of Cordelia, that is, of spiritual wisdom,[1] only the Fool is allowed to remain. He alone of them can fit into the new order because, although truly wise, he is wisdom masquerading as folly. Kent and Edgar can only return to the scene on similar conditions, the one disguised as a humble servant, the other as a lunatic beggar. If the opening scene stands for the Fall, the final events are an image, as we have seen, of *the promised end*, so that the period of the play may be said to span the whole cycle of time. This macrocosmic drama serves as a vast and shadowy backcloth for the story of a single individual soul.

The theme of *King Lear* as a drama of the microcosm is summed up in the following words from the King's speech:

> 'Tis our fast intent
> To shake all cares and business from our age,
> Conferring them on younger strengths, while we
> Unburthen'd crawl toward death.

These words mark the outset of his journey towards death, a journey which is to be soul-searchingly different from anything that he had imagined. In *The True Chronicle History of King Leir* which must have been, more than anything else, the source of Shakespeare's plot, the King speaks more humbly:

> The world of me, I of the world am weary
> And I would fain resign these earthly cares
> And think upon the welfare of my soul.

---

[1] There is a certain hierarchy to be observed among these characters, for Edgar is more nearly equal to Cordelia than the others are. In the sub-plot he is in fact her equivalent; and in the play as a whole, if she represents the transcendence of the Spirit, he may be said to stand for its immanence in this world. In *Measure for Measure* the Duke disguised corresponds to Edgar, the Duke as duke to Cordelia.

Shakespeare's Lear has too good an opinion of himself to express himself quite in these terms. His intention is indeed the same, that is, to be perfectly ready for death when death comes. Of that there can be no doubt, for Lear is deeply conscientious. But he clearly imagines that he has already more or less reached the necessary state. After so good and successful a life, what remains to be achieved between now and death? Surely it will be an easy, reposeful and agreeable passage, in the *kind nursery* of his favourite daughter Cordelia.

The first scene is a demonstration of his extreme unreadiness to die. From this microcosmic point of view the opening events do not represent the Fall itself but are as it were a re-enactment of the Fall. In other words, they serve as a sharp reminder of the fallenness of fallen man, and as such they mark the first step on the road to wisdom from out of a morass of blindness and indiscrimination in which Lear has long been stagnating. His fateful act at least serves to bring out into the open many of his faults, and although he does not recognize them as faults at the time he is able to do so later in retrospect. Regan speaks the truth for once when she says:

> *He hath ever but slenderly known himself.* (I, 1)

His previous life, before the play begins, has been a life of blindness as regards others also. He is quite ignorant of the true nature of his two elder daughters; and here again the sub-plot echoes the main plot, for Gloster is equally blind to the nature of his devilish bastard son Edmund, even to the point of not seeing his inferiority to Edgar. Lear does at least prefer Cordelia to her sisters:

> *I loved her most and thought to set my rest*
> *On her kind nursery.* (I, 1)

None the less, considering what Cordelia stands for, the very roots of all Lear's shortcomings may be said to lie in the superficiality of his love for her and his failure to rate her at her true worth. The Moor's love for Desdemona is lacking in light but not in warmth, whereas Lear's love for Cordelia is lacking in both. The light and the warmth are there, buried in the depth of the aged king's nature, and he discovers them later; but at the beginning of the play he both *sees* too little of Cordelia's inestimable value –

> *this unprized precious maid,*

as the King of France describes her – and *feels* too little a wrench in letting her go.

Cordelia, Edgar, Kent and the Fool are the embodiment of all goodness. Albany also has the same perfection, but it is not given the opportunity of manifesting itself until the play is drawing towards its end. The vices are personified by Goneril, Regan, Edmund and Cornwall. The devil is not represented by any one of these characters more than another, but his presence is felt in each of them as the root of all evil – a root which is often near to being laid bare. Between the two groups of uncompromising opposites stand the King and Gloster.

In *King Lear* as in *Hamlet* Hell and Purgatory are treated simultaneously which means that the discovery of hidden faults and the transformation of those faults into virtues go side by side. Lear's and Gloster's characters develop throughout the play. The virtues of spiritual poverty, humility, temperance, fidelity, love, kindness, discrimination and truth are developed against a background of worldly ambition, pride, anger, treachery, hatred, cruelty, blindness and untruth.

The descent into Hell is represented mainly in three different ways. Lear's discovery of the hitherto unsuspected faults of Goneril and Regan is like a mirror to reflect the discovery of the lower possibilities that lie hidden in his own soul; and in a sense Goneril and Regan are part of him. He says to Goneril:

> But yet thou are my flesh, my blood, my daughter;
> Or rather a disease that's in my flesh,
> Which I must needs call mine: thou art a boil,
> A plague-sore, an embossed carbuncle,
> In my corrupted blood.   (II, 4)

Secondly, as also in *Hamlet*, the state of the country reflects the soul of Everyman. In virtue of his kingship Lear *is* Britain; and he admits his responsibility in the words:

> O, I have ta'en too little care of this.   (II, 4)

As a supplement to the discovery of vices in Goneril and Regan the following speech of Lear from the storm scene may be quoted:

> Let the great gods
> That keep this dreadful pudder o'er our heads
> Find out their enemies now. Tremble, thou wretch,
> That hast within thee undivulged crimes,
> Unwhipp'd of justice; . . . close pent-up guilts,
> Rive your concealing continents and cry
> These dreadful summoners grace.   (III, 2)

Thirdly, Hell itself is as it were churned up on to the stage by Edgar. When he accuses himself of having been

> *false of heart, light of ear, bloody of hand, hog in*
> *sloth, fox in stealth, wolf in greediness, dog in madness,*
> *lion in prey* (III, 4)

it is not quite the same as when Hamlet says:

> *I could accuse me of such things that it were better*
> *my mother had not born me.* (III, 1)

In both cases the words are intended to throw light on the hidden evil in the soul of Everyman. But Hamlet's words refer directly to the speaker, whereas Edgar is not really accusing himself but holding out a mirror for Lear to look into. In fact, Edgar may be said to supply the 'scenery', the stage setting,[2] for Lear's descent into Hell. His ravings are equivalent to a procession of deadly sins and also a procession of devils, as he traces the human surfaces of evil to their infernal roots. Translated from the language of wildness to that of sobriety, the truth that he preaches without respite in the storm scene is that the state of fallen man is the state of being possessed, in some degree or other, by *the foul fiend, the prince of darkness.* In other words, as the Ghost in *Hamlet* puts it:

> *The serpent that did sting thy father's life*
> *Now wears his crown.* (I, 5)

Later Edgar 'demonstrates' to his father that it was not merely human initiative but above all the devil that had led him to the top of the cliff and tempted him to commit suicide, and that it was the grace of a divine intervention that had saved him:

> *Think that the clearest gods who make them honours*
> *Of men's impossibilities have preserved thee.* (IV, 6)

It is Edgar's function to dispel the illusion that man is independent and self-sufficient, and to show that his soul is largely a battleground for the forces of Heaven and Hell. We are especially reminded here, by contrast, of Iago's:

> *Virtue? A fig! 'Tis in ourselves that we are thus*
> *or thus,*

---

[2] In this sense, but in this sense alone, Edgar corresponds to the Porter in *Macbeth*.

a sentiment which Edmund would certainly have endorsed. Edgar is the
very opposite of his humanist brother.

Understanding of the nature of evil implies purification from evil,
and Edgar is not only a guide for the descent into Hell but also, much
more, a guide for the ascent of Purgatory. His occupation is, as he says:

> To prevent the foul fiend and to kill vermin   (III, 4)

that is, to kill those things in the soul that are purely negative and to
outwit the devil as regards such psychic substance as can be salvaged and
transformed. The inextricable interpenetration of Hell and Purgatory is
reflected not only in Edgar but also in the storm, which both voices the
anger of Heaven and purifies by the elements.

The deeper Lear descends into the abyss of Hell, the higher he
ascends up the mountain of Purgatory. But the ascent is gradual; he is
slow to see any parallel between Goneril's and Regan's treatment of him
and his treatment of Cordelia. There is one moment, just as he is setting
out from Goneril's house when he starts a sentence, half speaking to
himself, with the words *I did her wrong*, (I, 5) which would seem to refer to
Cordelia. But he evidently stifles any regrets that may have risen up in
him, and goes on almost immediately to speak of himself as *so kind a
father*; and even so late as the storm scene when, in an already quoted
speech, he invokes the Gods:

> Find out your enemies now

and adds:

> Tremble, thou wretch,
> That hast within thee undivulged crimes

he ends with the words of injured innocence:

> I am a man
> More sinn'd against than sinning.   (III, 2)

None the less, this scene marks a milestone on his journey. As Kent has
said of the world in its worldliness, as represented by the royal court:

> Freedom lies hence and banishment is here;

and now the world, which itself is banishment, has banished Lear, which
means that he is virtually set free from the numerous worldly ties with
which his soul was trussed. He had come to be altogether wrapped up in
himself. His extreme subjectivity now begins to unfold beneath the

humbling and universalizing power of the storm into an outlook that is more objective. When Kent suggests that he take shelter in a nearby hovel – which unknown to them is Edgar's hovel and therefore, symbolically, a palace of wisdom – Lear turns to the rain-drenched and shivering Fool and says:

> *Come on, my boy. How dost, my boy? Art cold? ...*
> *Poor fool and knave, I have one part in my heart*
> *That's sorry yet for thee.*

And when they reach the hovel and Kent begs him to enter, the King says:

> *Poor naked wretches, wheresoe'oer you are,*
> *That bide the pelting of this pitiless storm*
> *How shall your houseless heads and unfed sides,*
> *Your loop'd and window'd raggedness, defend you*
> *From seasons such as these? O! I have ta'en*
> *Too little care of this.* (III, 4)

But the effect of the storm on Lear is perhaps brought home to us more intimately in a later scene when he says in retrospect, giving us a glimpse of the latter part of his life, the years which led up to the opening scene of the play:

> *They flattered me like a dog, and told me I had*
> *white hairs in my beard ere the black ones were*
> *there. To say 'ay' and 'no' to every thing I said! ...*
> *When the rain came to wet me once and the wind to*
> *make me chatter, when the thunder would not peace*
> *at my bidding, there I found 'em, there I smelt 'em*
> *out. Go to, they are not men of their words: they*
> *told me I was everything: 'tis a lie, I am not*
> *ague-proof.* (IV, 6)

The freedom gained by banishment from the world is personified by Edgar in the extremity of his destitution. As Lear says to him:

> *Thou owest the worm no silk, the beast no hide, the*
> *sheep no wool, the cat no perfume. Ha! here's three on's are*
> *sophisticated; thou art the thing itself; unaccommodated man*
> *is no more but such a poor bare, forked animal as thou art.*
> *Off, off, you lendings!* (III, 4)

and he begins to tear off his own clothes. Shakespeare cannot quote here 'Blessed are the poor in spirit', but this beatitude was no doubt in his mind. Tradition the world over teaches that spiritual poverty, that is detachment from worldly things, was a spontaneous and outstanding attribute of man in his original perfection; and in all mysticisms the regaining of human perfection is conceived as a return to that primordial state. This aspect of human perfection loomed very large on Shakespeare's horizon. He was altogether exempt from that superstitious respect for civilization – 'sophistication', as Lear calls it – which has more or less dominated the West since his time and which now dominates almost the entire world. It would not be too much to say that he was haunted by the Golden Age. This comes out partly in his great reverence for virgin nature which is seen explicitly in *As You Like It, Cymbeline* and *The Tempest* and implicitly in many passages from other plays and in particular from *King Lear*; but it comes out above all in the fact that his ideal is always no less than the primordial ideal. In other words, his hero is not merely priest and not merely king, but the priest-king who alone is the true and rightful lord of virgin nature. Apart from those characters who personify this ideal from the outset – the banished Duke, for example, in *As You Like It*, Belarius in *Cymbeline*, Prospero in *The Tempest* and, without the primordial setting, the Duke of Vienna in *Measure for Measure* and Duncan, Malcolm and the briefly mentioned Edward the Confessor in *Macbeth* – the development which takes place in Hamlet's character might be summed up by saying that he has to realize fully the priest-kingship of which we are conscious as a virtuality in his nature from the very start. Might it not also be said that what is needed to make Othello perfect is the addition of a priestly element to his outstanding royalty of nature? As to *King Lear*, it is clearly the unfolding priesthood of the King which makes him sense the hidden bond between himself and Edgar – his *philosopher* as he calls him; and his *wits begin to turn* as if by spiritual contagion, as if he had 'caught' madness from Edgar.

Lear's madness is exactly parallel to Gloster's blindness, and Gloster's remark:

I stumbled when I saw

can be applied to Lear as much as to say that he blundered when he was sane. For just as Gloster's blindness marks the beginning of his path to true insight (it is at the moment of being blinded that he learns how he has been deceived by Edmund), so the turning of Lear's wits marks the unlocking of a door that opens onto wisdom. The difference between Edgar's 'madness' and Lear's madness only concerns the literal meaning of the play. Symbolically both represent turning one's back on worldly wisdom and embracing spiritual wisdom. The King's attitude towards Edgar is at first that of a novice towards an adept; but in his later mad scene, just before he is discovered by the search party sent out by Cordelia, he is no longer a novice and is able, like Edgar, to preach to Gloster:

> *Thou must be patient. We came crying hither:*
> *Thou knows't the first time that we smell the air*
> *We waul and cry. I will preach to thee; mark:*
> *When we are born, we cry that we are come*
> *To this great stage of fools.* (IV, 6)

The re-entry of Cordelia means a reversion to the normal order of things. So long as she was still present, in the first scene of the play, Lear's lack of wisdom appeared like the folly that is was. Kent had said:

> *Be Kent unmannerly*
> *When Lear is mad . . . To plainness honour's bound*
> *When majesty stoops to folly.*

It is therefore quite consequent that when Lear is once more in Cordelia's presence, his new-found wisdom should show as wisdom, not as folly, and that on being reunited with her he should recover his sanity. But at the moment of change from madness to sanity when Lear opens his eyes and sees Cordelia for the first time since their separation, Shakespeare takes advantage of the King's bewilderment in order to express directly the deeper meaning of this encounter which is no less than a heavenly visitation to a soul in Purgatory. Cordelia is, in virtue of what she symbolizes, definitely not of this world. The King says to her:

> *Thou art a soul in bliss; but I am bound*
> *Upon a wheel of fire, that mine own tears*
> *Do scald like molten lead . . .*
> *You are a spirit, I know.* (IV, 7)

Moreover, Lear is echoing here something of what the audience themselves have already felt when they for their part first see Cordelia again after so long and terrible an interval. Her sudden appearance when she enters as Queen of France and sends out soldiers to search the countryside for her father is for us also as though a piece of Heaven had descended to earth. This is a striking example, though not the only example, of Shakespeare's ability to achieve an overwhelming impact without the aid of words. We have not seen Cordelia since the first scene of the play. Meantime the vices of Goneril and Regan have been dug down to their hellish roots, and this has prompted us, if only subconsciously, to go through the opposite process with regard to Cordelia's virtues. As a result the contrast between the two elder sisters and the third sister has become so tremendous that this unexpected and almost unhoped for return is indescribably moving.

Lear has first of all the Fool for guide; then he is passed on from him to Edgar, and then from Edgar to Cordelia who, when her father's Purgatory is almost at an end, comes to give him a foretaste of Paradise and with it a foretaste of human perfection. That perfection, compounded of humility, love and wisdom, with the stress, as regards this last virtue, on discrimination, detachment and contemplative objectivity, the opposite of Lear's former undiscriminating, undetached and feverish subjectivity, comes to flower in his speech to Cordelia after they have lost the battle:

> Come, let's away to prison;
> We two alone will sing like birds i' the cage:
> When thou dost ask me blessing, I'll kneel down,
> And ask of thee forgiveness: so we'll live,
> And pray, and sing, and tell old tales, and laugh
> At gilded butterflies, and hear poor rogues
> Talk of court news; and we'll talk with them too
> Who loses and who wins; who's in, who's out.
> And take upon's the mystery of things
> As if we were God's spies; and we'll wear out
> In a wall'd prison, packs and sects of great ones
> That ebb and flow by the moon.   (V, 3)

It is the fully grown priest-king who then expresses his debt to Cordelia in the words:

> Upon such sacrifices, my Cordelia,
> The gods themselves throw incense.

Nor is it possible that Shakespeare has not in mind here, though he has to disguise his thought by the plural 'gods', the sacrifice which is, for the Western world, the very archetype of all sacrifice. The parallel is not remote, for in the first scene the King of France had said to Cordelia:

Thou losest here a better where to find,

and her sacrifice is that she has left that 'better where' for an incomparably 'worse where' in order that a man – who stands here for Everyman – might be saved.

In Cordelia the veil of humanity which hides the Spirit is almost transparent. She is not only incorruptible but also undeceivable.

I know you what you are;
And like a sister am most loth to call
Your faults as they are nam'd,

she says to her sisters in the first scene. She is also, in a sense, unassailable, like an impregnable fortress. While living in the world she has a hermit's detachment from it. One of her most significant remarks is the one which leads up to Lear's words about sacrifice. She says, when he begs her not to weep:

For thee oppressed king I am cast down.
Myself could else outfrown false fortune's frown.

The meaning of this second line is: As far as I myself am concerned, having passed judgement upon this world as the domain of ever-changing, fickle, unreliable fortune, I am always ready to frown on it, for what it is in general, with a frown far more severe than could be merited by any frown it could give me in the form of some particular piece of ill fortune.

Why does Shakespeare deliberately make Lear and Cordelia die, whereas Leir and Cordella are left alive at the end of the older play? The deepest reason of all is no doubt what is called 'poetic justice', which is partly the theme of a later chapter. Another more obvious reason, also deep yet easier to analyze, is that the old and broken Lear cannot represent the soul in its immortal union with the Spirit. Lear must therefore die into life, and where he is, there must Cordelia be. His reunion with her before the battle is only a foretaste; but in it there is, as we have seen, a hint of the true nature of the union as it will be when it is complete, for at first he thinks that they are both dead and that Cordelia is a blessed spirit; and at the end there is the strongest possible suggestion of the life after death. In a play like *King Lear* the dead cannot be made to speak. The King, when once he is dead, cannot get up and say: 'I now know that life is death and death is life'. But when he is on the very threshold of death – so near to being across that threshold that we can take what he says as news of the next world rather than of this – he tells us, almost in so many words, that Cordelia is alive. He had already said, before he was quite certain of her death, that if she be alive:

> *It is a chance which does redeem all sorrows*
> *That ever I have felt.*

But then he saw for certain, beyond any possible doubt, that she was dead:

> *No, no, no life!*
> *Why should a dog, a horse, a rat have life,*
> *And thou no breath at all? Thou'lt come no more,*
> *Never, never, never, never, never.*

Yet now, with his last breath, he says:

> *Do you see this? Look on her, look, her lips,*
> *Look there, look there!*

Bradley took these last words as an indication that Lear's actual death was due to the sudden joy of thinking that Cordelia was alive. I agree with him in being certain that these words can mean nothing other than that Cordelia is alive and that Lear dies in a state of bliss. But all things considered, is it not more likely that the chain of causility is the other way round? It was not because he saw (or thought he saw) that Cordelia was alive that he died; it was because he was dead (or as good as dead) that he saw she was alive – alive not with this life, but with the life after death.

CHAPTER 9

ANTONY AND CLEOPATRA

In three of his tragedies, *Romeo and Juliet*, *Othello*, and *Antony and Cleopatra*, Shakespeare combines the symbolism of marriage with the symbolism of death. In none of these three plays is the marriage really complete before death. In *Antony and Cleopatra* it is the nuptial bond itself that is lacking. Cleopatra, about to die, addresses the dead Antony with the words:

> *Husband, I come.*
> *Now to that name my courage prove my title.*[1]

In *Romeo and Juliet*, as in *Othello*, the lovers are in fact husband and wife, but they are allowed no peace and security together this side of the grave. Romeo and Juliet are married in secret and after one night together – a night spent in fear of discovery – they are separated. The rebirth and fulfilment of marriage after death are suggested by Romeo's dream of which he tells us just before the news comes to him of Juliet's death:

> *I dreamt my lady came and found me dead; –*
> *Strange dream, that gives a dead man leave to think –*
> *And breath'd such life with kisses in my lips,*
> *That I reviv'd, and was an emperor.*   (v. 1)

The union is further suggested by their being buried together in one tomb, as are Antony and Cleopatra.

---

[1] Let my courage, in dying for your sake, prove that I have a right to call you husband.

One of the differences between *Othello* and the other two tragedies is implicit in the singleness of the title. We have here the story of the Moor, not of his wife. He as Everyman represents the soul and she, perfect from the outset and having to undergo no process of development, represents the Spirit. There can be no question here of reversing the symbolism, whereas in *Antony and Cleopatra*, as we shall see on examining the text in more detail, each of the lovers has a double aspect, according to whether the play be considered as the story of Antony or the story of Cleopatra. If Cleopatra be taken as the more central figure, then it is she who represents the soul, while Antony, apotheosized after his death, symbolizes the Spirit, whereas for Antony as Everyman, the Spirit is symbolized by the Queen of Egypt.

But can the same be said, analogously, of *Romeo and Juliet*? The following quotation may help us to an answer, and it is less of a digression than it might at first seem:

> The marriage of sulphur and quicksilver, sun and moon, king and queen, is alchemy's central symbol, and in the light of its meaning we can clearly distinguish between alchemy and mysticism . . . The starting point of mysticism is that the soul has alienated itself from God through turning itself towards the world and that it must be reunited with Him . . . Alchemy on the other hand takes the standpoint that through the loss of his primordial 'Adamic' state, man is rent with inward discord, and can only regain his full being when the two powers whose strife has robbed him of his strength have been reconciled with each other. Human nature's inward dividedness, which has become as it were organic, is moreover a result of its having fallen away from God, inasmuch as it was the Fall which first made Adam and Eve aware of their opposition and thrust them out into the vicious circle of generation and death. Conversely man's winning back of his full nature, which alchemy expresses through the image of the male-female Hermaphrodite, is a necessary prelude to union with God though it may also be considered from another point of view as a fruit of that union . . .
>
> The marriage of the soul's masculine and feminine forces ultimately opens out onto the marriage of Spirit and soul . . . which is none other than the mystical marriage. Thus the two states overlap: the realization of psychic plenitude leads to the soul's giving itself to the Spirit, and the alchemical symbols have, correspondingly, more than one meaning: the sun and the moon can denote the two powers of the soul which are termed sulphur and quicksilver; at the same time they are images of the Spirit and the soul . . .
>
> Closely connected with the symbolism of marriage is the symbolism of death: according to some representations of the 'chemical marriage' the king and queen are killed at their wedding and buried together, thence to rise up rejuvenated.[2]

[2] Titus Burckhardt, *Alchemy*, pp.149, 155-6 (Stuart & Watkins, 1967).

If *Romeo and Juliet* were the only play of Shakespeare's that had come down to us, and if in the light of the above quotation we were called upon to answer the question: 'Is the symbolism of *Romeo and Juliet* mystical or alchemical?', there would be a strong case for replying that it is alchemical, the more so in that the two lovers are as it were transmuted into gold after their deaths, for Romeo's father says:

> *I will raise her statue in pure gold*

and Juliet's father replies:

> *As rich shall Romeo by his lady lie.*

Moreover, the strife between the two powers of the soul would seem to be adequately represented by the enmity between the houses of Montagu and Capulet, an enmity which is at the end transformed into friendship. On the other hand there can be no doubt that the symbolism of the maturer plays is mystical, love having here a higher significance expressive of the relationship between soul and Spirit; and apart from what has already been said about *Othello* and *King Lear*, a clear indication of this higher symbolism is to be found in the presence of Juno and Ceres, representing Heaven and earth, that is, Spirit and soul, at the betrothal of Ferdinand and Miranda in *The Tempest*. Needless to say, Shakespeare could have changed his perspective in the approximately ten year interval between *Romeo and Juliet* and *Othello*. But a closer examination of the text shows that his ultimate outlook was already, to say the least, well on its way to being formed when he wrote the earlier play, and the metal gold is here without doubt a symbol of the Spirit which each of the lovers represents for the other, as in *Antony and Cleopatra*, and which each, through death, has now actually become.

There is nothing strange or forced in this reversible relationship between the two lovers. Symbolism is not arbitrary, but is based on the very nature of things, on the make-up of the universe. According to all cosmological and metaphysical doctrines, whether Eastern or Western, earthly phenomena are nothing other than the shadows or reflections of spiritual realities. The symbolism of a thing is its power to recall its higher reality, in the same way that a reflection or shadow can give us a fleeting glimpse of the object that casts it; and the best symbols – the only ones worthy to be used in sacred art – are those things which are most perfect of their kind, for they are the clearest reflections, the sharpest shadows, of the higher reality which is their archetype. One of the chief applications of this doctrine to mysticism is that every object of love is a symbol of the Divine Beauty of the Spirit and therefore has power to recall something of that Beauty. This explains why in all love worthy of the name there is always an element of worship. Love has always a double aspect: the beloved is loved for himself or herself and, beyond that, for the sake of the Reality in whose image man was created.

For Romeo *Juliet is the sun*; at their first encounter her hand is a *holy shrine*, she is a *saint* and he a *pilgrim*; and at the end the presence of her body transforms the burial vault to a *lantern*, that part of a cathedral which according to Masonic symbolism corresponds to Heaven and the Spirit. For Juliet, Romeo is the *god* of her *idolatry*.

The last words are tantamount to her saying of him, as he says of her, that he *is the sun*. If the symbolism were 'alchemical' in the narrower sense, he would be irreversibly the sun and she the moon, which is not the case. None the less, the alchemical marriage cannot be altogether excluded here, for whether it entered into Shakespeare's direct and immediate intention or not, he was fully aware that a symbol cannot be limited to one level only. Marriage is a symbol of all the complementary pairs which lie above it, whether the two terms of the pair are on the same level as in the case of the 'alchemical marriage', or one above the other as in the case of the mystical marriage of Spirit and soul; and although Shakespeare has this 'vertical' symbolism directly in mind, he would have known that when an artist uses a symbol it is as if he had set free a bird to fly in a certain direction without his being able to limit the extent of its flight, and that independently of his intention marriage necessarily symbolizes also, below its mystical significance, the perfect union of the active and passive aspects of the soul; and he would have known that above all, beyond the union of soul and Spirit, marriage is a symbol of the inseparable union of two complementary Qualities or Aspects of the Divinity Itself, for the Divine Beatitude, which is nothing other than God's Love for Himself, is the Supreme Archetype of all the complementary pairs in existence, just as each single thing has its Supreme Archetype in a single Divine Quality. In other words, a symbol is fraught with repercussions for the soul of man, and on the 'wings' of these repercussions the intuition may rise up through a series of higher realities in the direction of Absolute Reality, and it is precisely because symbols are the language of sacred art that a work of this art has different meanings at different levels.

In addition to its general symbolism, and despite the great outward differences, *Romeo and Juliet* has also some important details in common with *Antony and Cleopatra*. Each of the four lovers is called upon eventually to face the fact that the beloved can only be reached through the 'narrow gate' of death. The difficulty of placing all four in this same situation is overcome by the device of the false news which Romeo receives of Juliet's death and which Antony receives of Cleopatra's; and like the Moor of Venice, each of the four souls dies a self-inflicted death for the sake of being united with the beloved in the next world.

But is there no inconsistency between the conception of suicide in *Hamlet* and *King Lear* as a deadly sin, and the representation of the suicides of Romeo, Juliet, Othello, Antony and Cleopatra as noble acts? As regards the last three characters, the answer is undoubtedly 'No'. In *Hamlet* and *King Lear* suicide is considered in a purely literal sense. But where death is symbolic of the 'narrow gate' that leads to life, then of all manners of deaths suicide is one of the most powerfully symbolic, for it expresses most clearly the fact that the aspiring soul seeks its own death; and as regards *Antony and Cleopatra*, we must remember that suicide in certain circumstances was not only legitimate but even highly meritorious according to the more ancient religious perspectives. As to *Othello*, although the Moor is a Christian, he stands at the very fringe of Christendom. Consequently, it is not difficult for us to accept his suicide as an objective act of justice against himself in accordance with some law unknown to us. Moreover, if we recall the words of Edgar, '*ripeness is all*', Shakespeare makes us feel that Othello, like Antony and Cleopatra, is 'ripe' for death, that he has fully completed the course of his little earthly cycle, whereas when Hamlet thinks about suicide he is not 'ripe', neither is Gloster when he actually attempts it. In their case suicide would have been a revolt against destiny, but in the case of Othello we know that it is, on the contrary, an acceptance of destiny, the inescapability of which makes him cry out:

Who can control his fate?

There is nothing here, just as there is nothing in *Antony and Cleopatra*, to mar the effectiveness of suicide as a perfect symbol of the mystic's fully intentioned 'dying into life'. But in the earliest of these three plays Shakespeare has not fully succeeded in convincing us that either Romeo or Juliet is 'ripe' for death. Their tragedy is moreover set in the very heart of Christendom where it is impossible to forget that suicide is among the most deadly of sins.

It is to be suspected that Shakespeare was one of his own severest critics, and he must have been well aware of this shortcoming, at any rate in his later years. However that may be, and whether or not *Romeo and Juliet* was actually present in his mind when he wrote *Antony and Cleopatra*, it cannot be denied that he is at some pains in the later play to avoid what is, precisely, the fault of the earlier one, and he certainly succeeds.

But in all justice, it must be admitted that if we had to sacrifice one of these two plays, the choice would not be obvious. Nor would our hesitation be due to any inferiority or mediocrity in *Antony and Cleopatra* but rather to the overwhelming beauty of *Romeo and Juliet* as an expression of love. The perfecting of the Moor's love for Desdemona is the theme of *Othello* just as the perfecting of the love of Antony and Cleopatra for each other is the theme of the play we are now considering. But in *Romeo and Juliet* there is no comparable development of soul, and the play is largely centred on the tragic contrast between the extreme perfection of a love and the extreme imperfection of the circumstances it is set in. Consequently, Shakespeare is able to dwell throughout this earlier play on a perfection which is only reached at the end of the other two, with the result that if we simply compare the three as regards the element 'love', it is no doubt the love between Romeo and Juliet which has, as symbol, the strongest wings for the highest flights.

A striking feature of *Antony and Cleopatra* that we do not find in any other play of Shakespeare is that the outer or macrocosmic meaning runs contrary to the inner one. Normally the two meanings are parallel: Hamlet, for example, while representing the soul that seeks to restore the lost harmony of the inner world represents at the same time a man who seeks to restore the lost harmony of the outer world. But in *Antony and Cleopatra* according to the outer meaning it is Octavius Caesar who is in the right, so to speak, from the beginning of the play, and it is he who finally restores order in the capacity of *sole sire of the world* as Cleopatra calls him. This outer meaning becomes reconciled with the inner meaning at the very end of the play when Caesar pays a certain tribute of admiration to Antony and Cleopatra after their deaths. But throughout the course of the play the hero and heroine are both very much in the wrong according to the outer meaning, and they are mercilessly presented as being so from the start. The opening speech, which is all the more derogatory for being spoken by Philo who is one of Antony's friends, rings with scorn at Antony's besotted doting on a 'gypsy' who has made him completely forget his duty as Triumvir, one of the three rulers of 'the world'. Philo expresses here the general unhesitating and sweeping censure of Antony's conduct; and yet according to the play's deeper meaning – a meaning which is felt in some degree or other by every member of the audience – Antony's love for Cleopatra is the richest jewel of virtue in his soul. This opposition between the outer and inner meanings is itself symbolic, for it reflects the truth that the mysteries can only be understood by a few, or more generally, for those who know nothing of the mysteries, the truth that the majority are by no means always right and that the ways of Heaven are sometimes inscrutable.

Let us quote here a short passage starting from line 10 of the play, at the entry of Antony and Cleopatra:

Philo [to Dercetas]	*Look where they come:*
	Take but good note, and you shall see in him
	The triple pillar of the world transform'd
	Into a strumpet's fool: behold and see.
Cleopatra	*If it be love indeed, tell me how much.*
Antony	*There's beggary in the love that can be reckon'd.*
Cleopatra	*I'll set a bourn how far to be beloved.*
Antony	*Then thou must needs find out new heaven,*
	new earth.
Attendant [entering]	*News, my good Lord, from Rome.*
Antony	*Grates me: the sum.*[3]

And in the end Antony does not even listen to 'the sum' of the news, but goes off with Cleopatra.

In a sense the whole play is contained in these eight lines, at any rate that aspect of it according to which the soul is represented by Antony. Let us consider this aspect of the play first. Outwardly Rome stands for duty, sobriety and morality in general; it also stands for reason, and the dialogue abounds in powerful arguments why Antony should leave Egypt altogether – Egypt which spells neglect of duty, lack of sobriety, lack of moral principles and also the vanity of unreason. But this outer meaning does not constitute in any sense a morality play; it is like the thinnest of veils, which hides the truth from no one, although needless to say the truth is for the most part felt rather than analysed. What are the means by which, beneath this most transparent outside, Shakespeare contrives to weight the scales so heavily in favour of Egypt? One of the first things that comes to mind is the symbolism of East and West which correspond to Heaven and earth; and it is certainly not Rome which stands at the celestial point of the compass. Rome is this world, and nothing but this world – a down-to-earth well-being, social stability,

---

[3] It annoys me: give me a brief summary of it and no more.

and material security. And as Antony says, in the first scene of the play:

> *Kingdoms are clay: our dungy earth alike*
> *Feeds beast as man: the nobleness of life*
> *Is to do thus, when such a mutual pair*
> *And such a twain can do it.*

In other words the Roman Empire is a mere stretch of land. All that Rome stands for is that aspect of man wherein he merely has the virtue of being an animal rather a vegetable or a mineral. But the noblest aspect of life is the love that is felt between two perfectly matched lovers.

In the light of what the East stands for, Roman 'virtues' are no more than human limitations: Roman rationality is human intelligence deprived of its supra-rational, superhuman dimension; Roman morality is a system of ethics made to fit the shortcomings of that intelligence; Roman sobriety is a dismal lack of spiritual intoxication. Conversely, the 'vices' of Egypt amount to a breaking down of the barriers of human limitations. In Shakespeare's other representations of 'the pearl of great price', the Divine Qualities of the Spirit are symbolized by outstanding human virtues. But in this play the stress is on the Spirit's incomparability, the lack of any common measure between this world and the next; and as a symbol of the celestial, it is the function of Egypt to convey to us something of the next world's elusive mysteriousness that passes human comprehension, its infinite riches, its marvellous variety and its boundless freedom. Everything that Egypt stands for is personified by Cleopatra. Moreover, as Queen of Egypt she is virtually divine and we are told that it was her practice to give audience

> *In the habilments of the goddess Isis.*
>
> (III, 6)

From the point of view we are taking here it is only a glib and superficial judgement that will attribute faults to her. There is an elusive infallibility about her, a mysterious overall 'rightness' which transcends human rightness and defies criticism. Antony expresses this when he says:

> *Fie, wrangling queen!*
> *Whom everything becomes – to chide, to laugh.*
> *To weep.*   (I, 1)

And when it seems that Antony, newly betrothed to Octavia, has finished with Cleopatra, and when Maecenas says:

Now Antony must leave her utterly

Enobarbus replies:

> *Never, he will not:*
> *Age cannot wither her, nor custom stale*
> *Her infinite variety: other women cloy*
> *The appetites they feed: but she makes hungry*
> *Where most she satisfies; for vilest things*
> *Become themselves in her, that the holy priests*
> *Bless her when she is riggish.*   (II, 2)

There is also a cosmic, 'collective' quality about Cleopatra which bursts out beyond the bounds which limit the sphere of an ordinary single human individual, so that she is in some respects more a macrocosm than a microcosm. This is true in a sense of all monarchs, but what is more or less virtual in other kings and queens is actualized in Cleopatra to an outstanding degree. With her it is not merely a question of function. We are made to feel that her very psychic substance is macrocosmic. As Enobarbus says of her:

> *We cannot call her winds and waters sighs and*
> *tears; they are greater storms and tempests*
> *than almanacs can report.*   (I, 2)

Rich in implication also is Cleopatra's own remark when she is chided for unjustly striking the messenger who brings her the news of Antony's marriage:

> *Some innocents scape not the thunderbolt.*

Another aspect of this same quality is to be seen in the grandeur of her lavishness – which Rome would call extravagance – as when, on being asked why she sends so many messengers to Antony she replies:

> *Who's born that day*
> *When I forget to send to Antony*
> *Shall die a beggar. Ink and paper, Charmian...*
> *He shall have every day a several greeting,*
> *Or I'll unpeople Egypt.*   (I, 5)

These illustrations of aspects of the 'supernatural' in Cleopatra's nature are not all taken from the first scenes of the play. But the very concentrated first scene of all is quite enough to give us our orientation –

in the literal sense of the word. Consequently, no member of the
audience is misled when in the second scene Antony says:

> These strong Egyptian fetters I must break,
> Or lose myself in dotage . . .
> I must from this enchanting queen break off:
> Ten thousand harms, more than the ills I know,
> My idleness doth hatch.

We know that despite his logic Antony is here 'in the wrong' and that he
is expressing a kind of worldly escapism from his higher destiny. As far
as he is concerned the basic theme of this play, his Purgatory,[4] is the
perfecting of his devotion to Cleopatra. For this love to become whole-
hearted he needs to extricate his soul from worldly ties and to purge it
from the dross of 'Roman thoughts'. Apart from this his spiritual path
cannot be traced by any marked psychic development but simply by his
gradual worldly ruin. Perhaps the most significant milestone in this
development is when, for no logically justifiable cause, he suddenly
follows Cleopatra in flight from the Battle of Actium; the event is
described by Scarus, one of Antony's more devoted followers:

> The greatest cantle of the world is lost
> With very ignorance; we have kissed away
> Kingdoms and provinces . . .
> I never saw an action of such shame;
> Experience, manhood, honour, ne'er before
> Did violate so itself.   (III, 10)

There is symbolically an analogy between Lear's madness and Antony's
blundering; if we can say of Lear 'the madder the wiser', we can say of
Antony 'the more he fails the more he succeeds' or 'the weaker the
stronger' or 'the poorer the richer'; and this Antony himself confirms
when he says, after the battle, that one of Cleopatra's tears alone is
worth all that he has lost.

Antony's being purged of 'Roman thoughts' proceeds to the outward
accompaniment of his being deserted by Roman after Roman –
Canidius, Enobarbus, and others. This spiritual death – being stripped
of all worldly powers and possessions – is not without its death agonies;
as Charmian says:

---

[4] In this play the descent into Hell is merely implicit in the ascent through Purgatory.

> *The soul and body rive not more in parting*
> *Than greatness going off.*   (IV, 13)

In the most violent of these agonies Antony cries out:

> *The shirt of Nessus[5] is upon me: teach me,*
> *Alcides, thou mine ancestor, thy rage:*
> *Let me lodge Lichas on the horns of the moon;*
> *And with those hands, that grasped the heaviest*
>   *club,*
> *Subdue my worthiest self. The witch shall die:*
> *To the young Roman boy she has sold me, and I*
>   *fall*
> *Under this plot; she dies for't.*   (IV, 12)

It is natural that the dying soul should have its reaction against that which is killing it. The 'witch' in question, Cleopatra, is in fact the cause of Antony's worldly failure. None the less, his particular accusation is unjust, for there can be no doubt that she has not betrayed him. This brings us to another aspect of Antony's short-coming: one of the flaws in his devotion to Cleopatra is that like Othello he does not love wisely enough. He does not know Cleopatra as well as he should.

> *Not know me yet?*   (III, 13)

[5] The centaur Nessus sent Hercules (Alcides), Antony's ancestor, a poisoned shirt. Hercules, dying in agony, hurled Lichas, who had brought the shirt, up to the sky, and then put an end to his own life. Although outwardly the cause is quite different, Hamlet's outburst against Laertes at the burial of Ophelia (see p.38, note), his last show of weakness, is also a kind of death agony, and corresponds exactly to this outburst of Antony in that it marks the same point upon the spiritual path. Hamlet, like Antony, realizes that he has been utterly stripped of this world; and both outbursts have much in common as regards what might be called the magnificent extravagance of their imagery. Hamlet 'rants' (to use his own word):

> *I loved Ophelia; forty thousand brothers*
> *Could not, with all their quantity of love,*
> *Make up my sum. − What wilt thou do for her? . . .*
> *Woul't weep? woul't fight? woul't fast? woul't tear thyself?*
> *Woul't drink up eisel? eat a crocodile?*
> *I'll do't. − Dost thou come here to whine?*
> *To outface me with leaping in her grave?*
> *Be buried quick with her, and so will I:*
> *And, if thou prate of mountains, let them throw*
> *Millions of acres on us, till our ground,*
> *Singeing his pate against the burning zone,*
> *Make Ossa like a wart!*   (V, 1)

she complains when, not for the last time, he loses faith in her and accuses her of betraying him. He can be excused for not knowing her as well as she knows him, because she has about her an enigmatic inscrutability which together with her extreme acuteness of perception is part of her 'transcendence'. But his liability to lose faith in her – he does so twice towards the end of the play – is symbolically as inexcusable as the weakness of losing faith in religion which can also be inscrutable.

When his final rage subsides, it leaves him at the extreme limit of poverty, that is, at the very verge of extinction and nothingness:

Antony	*Eros, thou yet behold'st me?*
Eros	*Ay, noble Lord.*
Antony	*Sometime we see a cloud that's dragonish,*
	A vapour sometime like a bear or lion,
	A tower'd citadel, a pendent rock,
	A forked mountain, or blue promontory
	With trees upon't, that nod unto the world
	And mock our eyes with air: thou hast seen these signs;
	They are black vesper's pageants.
Eros	*Ay, my Lord.*
Antony	*That which is now a horse, even with a thought,*
	The rack dislimns, and makes it indistinct
	As water is in water.
Eros	*It does, my Lord.*
Antony	*My good knave Eros, now thy captain is*
	Even such a body; here I am Antony;
	Yet cannot hold this visible shape, my knave. (IV, 14)

The 'false' news which then comes of Cleopatra's death is really a truth in disguise, and it is so in a double sense: it teaches Antony the truth that she belongs to the next world, not this, and that he can only be united with her by himself passing through death; and it also 'proves' to him beyond any doubt that she is altogether faithful to him, so that when he deals himself the wound he is to die of, his love is no longer lacking in wisdom. His situation at this moment is very similar in almost every respect to that of the Moor at the close of *Othello*.

At the moment where the story of Antony ends, the story of the pilgrimage of Cleopatra comes into the foreground. The spiritual aspect of Antony has been present in the background throughout, and has come once or twice into the foreground, especially in the scene where Alexas brings a pearl from him to Cleopatra who says:

> *How much unlike thou art Mark Antony!*
> *Yet, coming from him, that great medicine*[6] *hath*
> *With his tinct gilded thee.*   (I, 5)

We may quote also from the same scene:

Cleopatra	*What, was he sad or merry?*
Alexas	*Like to the time o' the year between the extremes*
	Of hot and cold, he was nor sad nor merry.
Cleopatra	*O well-divided disposition! Note him . . .*
	He was not sad, for he would shine on those
	Who make their looks by his; he was not merry,
	Which seem'd to tell them his rememberance lay
	In Egypt with his joy; but between both:
	O heavenly mingle! Be'est thou sad or merry,
	The violence of either thee becomes,
	So does it no man else.

This scene prepares us for the conversation between Cleopatra and Dolabella in the last scene of the play, that is, after Antony's death.

Cleopatra	*I dreamt there was an Emperor Antony:*
	O! such another sleep, that I might see
	But such another man! . . .
	His face was as the heavens; and therein stuck
	A sun and moon, which kept their course, and lighted
	The little O, the earth . . .
	His legs bestrid the ocean: his rear'd arm
	Crested the world: his voice was propertied
	As all the tuned spheres, and that to friends;
	But when he meant to quail and shake the orb
	He was as rattling thunder. For his bounty,
	There was no winter in't; an autumn 'twas
	That grew the more by reaping . . .
	Think you there was, or might be, such a man
	As this I dreamt of?
Dolabella	*Gentle madam, no.*
Cleopatra	*You lie, up to the hearing of the gods.*

---

[6] The Philosopher's Stone which, having power to transmute baser metals into gold, is an image of the Divine Spirit.

The alternative which faced Antony throughout the whole play, the choice between Heaven and earth, the celestial East and the worldly West, and which is finally forced on him by the 'false' news of Cleopatra's death, is also brought home to Cleopatra by Antony's death. But for her the symbol vanishes into the reality; the choice is not between Egypt and Rome but quite literally between Heaven and earth. It now faces her for the first time; until then, as she says,

> It were for me
> To throw my sceptre at the injurious gods;
> To tell them that this world did equal theirs
> Till they had stol'n our jewel. All's but naught;
> Patience is sottish and impatience does
> Become a dog that's mad.

The word 'injurious' does not make Cleopatra's remark comparable to Gloster's

> As flies to wanton boys are we to the gods:
> They kill us for their sport.

She does not need Edgar to tell her that *impatience does become a dog that's mad*. Her attitude is as much intellectual as sentimental. Now that Antony, a brief loan from Heaven to earth which she never really possessed, has been snatched back, she sees this world as utter vanity.

> And there is nothing left remarkable
> Beneath the visiting moon.

Both patience and impatience are equally pointless. The situation is for her as a Divine summons to the next world.

In the following scene, the last of the play, she continues in the same vein:

> My desolation does begin to make
> A better life. 'Tis paltry to be Caesar;
> Not being Fortune, he's but Fortune's knave,
> A minister of her will: and it is great
> To do that thing that ends all other deeds;
> Which shackles accidents and bolts up change;
> Which sleeps, and never palates more the dung,
> The beggar's nurse and Caesar's.

In the first scene of the play Antony had already said:

> *Our dungy earth alike*
> *Feeds beast as man.*

None the less, to kill herself is, for Cleopatra, the most difficult thing in the world – as difficult as it is for Isabella to forego her revenge on Angelo. There is nothing at all of the European romantic about Cleopatra. She has a deep-rooted Oriental practicality and no one needs less to be taught the old adage that warns us against putting all our eggs into one basket. Earlier on, when Caesar's messenger suggested to her that her attitude to Antony was one of fear rather than of love, she agreed with him for no other reason, apparently, than because she could not bear to throw away a possible advantage. Might it not be very useful to her in the future that Caesar should have such ideas in his head about her relationship with Antony? It was not for nothing that in a previous scene Antony had said of her:

> *She is cunning past man's thought.*

And now, when she is overflowing with contempt for this world and when she has already decided, so it seems, to put an end to her life, she is none the less prepared to go to some lengths in order to prevent Caesar from laying hands on the bulk of her treasure. Her treasurer's betrayal of her perhaps helps her to make up her mind altogether and overcome her last lingering weaknesses. In view of these weaknesses, in view of the fact that to kill herself is, for her, the most difficult thing in the world, suicide is in her case, doubly symbolic: it means both killing 'the dragon' and passing through the 'narrow gate' and as such it is equivalent both to Hamlet's killing Claudius and to his dying himself.
    When singleness of purpose finally crystallizes in her, she says:

> *Show me, my women, like a queen: go fetch*
> *My best attires: I am again for Cydnus*
> *To meet Mark Antony.*

and then:

> *Give me my robe, put on my crown; I have*
> *Immortal longings in me: now no more*
> *The juice of Egypt's grape shall moist this lip...*
>   *Husband, I come:*
> *Now to that name my courage prove my title!*
> *I am fire and air; my other elements*
> *I give to baser life.*

Previously Antony had said, in just the same situation:

> *I come, my queen . . . stay for me*
> *Where souls do couch on flowers we'll hand in hand,*
> *And with our sprightly port make the ghosts gaze . . .*
>   *I will be*
> *A bridegroom in my death, and run into't*
> *As to a lover's bed.*   (IV, 14)

CHAPTER 10

CYMBELINE

In the *Divine Comedy*, shortly before Dante reaches the top of the Mountain of Purgatory, he is made to pass through the fire, fire which harms not a hair of his head yet which is so fierce to the senses that – to use his own image – if there had been a vat of molten glass at hand he would have plunged into it to cool himself. After this there remains no further obstacle between him and the top of the mountain on which is the Garden of Eden. But the night has fallen, and so, unable to go any further, he lies down to sleep; and in that sleep he dreams of the Earthly Paradise which he is to enter the next day.

In all the plays we have considered so far except *Macbeth*, Shakespeare takes his heroes and heroines up the Mountain of Purgatory and through the final fire to that sleep, and sometimes to that dream of Paradise; but he takes them no further. Even at the end of *Measure for Measure* we are, as it were, only upon the threshold. As to the other great plays of this so-called 'middle' period, they are in any case all tragedies and as such could at the most only imply or herald what lies beyond Purgatory, without directly representing it on the stage. But in the latest of these, *Antony and Cleopatra*, Shakespeare's treatment of his theme comes near to bursting the tragic form and to overflowing across the threshold of Paradise. It is therefore not surprising that for his last plays, *Pericles, Cymbeline, The Winter's Tale* and *The Tempest*, he should have abandoned that form for one which would allow him to express directly not merely Purgatory itself, but also something of what Purgatory leads to.

The opening situation of *Cymbeline* reminds us, in different ways, both of *Hamlet* and of *Othello*. Daughter and father in *Cymbeline* correspond to son and mother in *Hamlet*. Cymbeline himself, like Gertrude, represents the passive aspect of the human soul in its state of fallenness, and Imogen, like the Prince of Denmark, represents the active aspect of the soul, its conscience and its intelligence. The soul's state of corruption is indicated by Cymbeline's second marriage, his being dominated by his *wicked queen* as he calls her at the end, just as in *Hamlet* it is indicated by Gertrude's marriage to Claudius. For the rest, the same truths are expressed in each play, but by means of different symbols. In *Hamlet* the Fall is marked by the murder of Gertrude's first husband, which brought about the soul's separation from the Spirit. In *Cymbeline* it is not represented by the death of the King's first wife, which is not mentioned, but by the loss of his 'immortality', that is, by the loss of his two sons, the result of his misguided rupture with his wise counsellor Belarius. Unlike Cordelia, Imogen is not enhanced as a symbol through being the King's third child. It is only at the very end of the play that the number three comes into its own when Cymbeline, having regained all his children, speaks of himself as being

A mother to the birth of three.

Until then it is the number two, in its positive aspect, which takes precedence. The King's two elder children represent here the two natures, heavenly and earthly, of primordial man. Fallen man, by comparison, is single, with a singleness of nature which is at the same time fragmentary, inasmuch as the remaining earthly nature is no longer perfect as it was before; and Cymbeline is reduced to that fragmentary singleness by being left with only a daughter, that is, with something less good, from the point of view of succession, than a single son would have been. The two sons are *the two worlds*, Heaven and earth, which Imogen (including her father) regains at the end of the play. She says:

I have got two worlds by't,

that is, by the return of her two brothers. Their presence at her final union with Posthumus is thus exactly equivalent to the presence of Juno and Ceres at the betrothal of Miranda and Ferdinand; and although the symbolism of *The Winter's Tale* is not strengthened by any such presence, it is significant that Leontes at least mentions the two worlds in question when he says, of the newly betrothed Perdita and Florizel:

> *I lost a couple, that 'twixt heaven and earth*
> *Might thus have stood, begetting wonder as*
> *You, gracious couple, do.*   (v.1)

The significance of Cymbeline's two sons is thus the same as that of Castor and Pollux,[1] and it seems almost certain that Shakespeare had the heavenly twins in mind here, for he makes Balarius say of the two princes:

> *They are worthy*
> *To inlay the heaven with stars.*   (v, 5)

and at the end Cymbeline prays that they may continue to *reign* in their *orbs*. They are also, like Antony, the Philosopher's Stone, for like *that great medicine*[2] they too have power to turn baser metals into gold, inasmuch as they are spoken of as having *gilded pale looks* in the battle. Relatively speaking both the brothers, and not merely one, may be called 'heavenly' because the earth which the second brother signifies is not the earth as it is but as it was primordially, a Paradise altogether penetrated with celestial influences.

The symbolism of the two brothers calls for no less than the perfection which in fact they have; and this brings us to a point which concerns Shakespeare's last plays in general. These plays are less naturalistic and more medieval not only in virtue of the presence of Divine Powers albeit necessarily in 'pagan' disguise – Diana in *Pericles*, Jupiter in *Cymbeline*, Apollo in *The Winter's Tale* and Juno, Iris and Ceres in *The Tempest* – but also through the relative absence of psychological detail in the characters, an absence which is made up for by detail of another kind. It is to be noticed, for example, that in the three latest plays, those persons who represent the lost spiritual wisdom are not only perfect in character, like Desdemona and Cordelia, but also perfect in the circumstances of their lives; the two sons of Cymbeline have been brought up amid entirely natural surroundings, far away from all contact with corrupt civilization; Perdita has been brought up by shepherds

---

[1] The heavenly twins were born from an egg that was laid by Leda, having been engendered by Jupiter in the form of a swan. René Guénon in *La Grande Triade* (La Table Ronde, 1946, p.43) remarks that in Hinduism, to which the ancient Greek tradition is related, the creation of the universe is represented by the hatching of a swan's egg out of the two halves of which come heaven and earth. The swan is here the symbol of the Spirit of God which 'breathed upon the face of the waters': and the 'dividing of the waters' in Genesis is equivalent to the dividing of the 'egg of the Universe' in Hinduism.

[2] See above, p.95, note.

whose way of life has always been associated with purity and innocence; and Miranda has been brought up on the enchanted island.

What the openings of *Cymbeline* and *Othello* have in common is that in both plots the powers of darkness had been scheming to bring the soul of Everyman still further under their domination. Iago had been doing his utmost to have himself appointed as the Moor's lieutenant; and in *Cymbeline* the wicked step-mother had been doing her utmost to marry Imogen to her son Cloten. In both cases the devil has failed to increase his hold upon his victim; and what is more, a sudden and secret marriage between soul and Spirit has taken him altogether by surprise.

Posthumus is an eagle –

> *I chose an eagle,*
> *And did avoid a puttock.*[3] (I, 1)

says Imogen – and he is also Leonatus, *the lion's whelp*, the eagle and the lion being the bird and beast of the sun which is the great symbol of the Spirit. There is no common measure, from this point of view, between Leonatus and Imogen, since he, as she says,

> *overbuys me*
> *Almost the sum he pays.*   (*ibid.*)

and since Iachimo in the hour of repentance describes Posthumus as being

> *The best of all*
> *Amongst the rarest of good ones.*   (V, 5)

we may quote also as sincere in his earlier remark:

> *He sits 'mongst men like a descended god.*   (I, 6)

But in *Cymbeline*, as in *Othello*, the marriage is only virtual. It has not yet been consummated, and does not become fully actualized until the very end. Posthumus is immediately banished; and by banishing him, the king in a sense re-enacts the Fall, reiterating the loss of his two sons. The complete reversal of the situation at the end is indicated by Cymbeline's taking a lesson from Posthumus, who has just pronounced his forgiveness of Iachimo. Cymbeline says:

---

[3] Kite.

Nobly doomed!
We'll learn our freeness of a son-in-law;
Pardon's the word to all.

And Posthumus's symbolic identity with the King's two sons is
confirmed by their joyful acceptance of him as a brother.

Although, as we have seen, the relationship between Imogen and her
father corresponds globally to the relationship between Hamlet and his
mother, there is a considerable difference of detail. In *Hamlet* both the
Prince and the Queen share the imperfection of fallen man and both
have to develop and be purified. In *Cymbeline* all the faults are
concentrated in the King, who remains entirely static, his only
development being his repentance. Imogen personifies fallen man's
better nature struggling to free itself. Unlike Hamlet she is represented
as being perfect from the start, her only imperfection being that she is
not yet free. The spiritual path is her escape from the court and her
journey to Milford Haven in order to make good her marriage. This
journey is a perfect image of the 'straightened way which leadeth unto
life'; and it is so fraught with destitution and desolation that she may
be said to have passed through the narrow gate of death. It is significant
that when she is finally found by the Roman Lucius she replies, in
answer to his question who she is:

I am nothing; or if not
Nothing to be were better.[4]   (IV, 2)

But on the journey she has been given a foretaste of Paradise in her
fleeting reunion with her two lost brothers. Here again the symbolic
identity between them and Posthumus is brought out, for they take as it
were his place in Imogen's eyes, and although she does not know who
they are, she momentarily transfers her allegiance from him to them,
since he has forsaken her.

Pardon me, gods!
I'ld change my sex to be companion with them,
Since Leonatus false.   (III, 7)

Meantime other effects of her spiritual striving are to be seen, not in
herself where there is no room for development, but in that part of the
soul which is directly dominated by the powers of darkness. These

---

[4] It would be better to be nothing than what I am.

powers are gradually being forced to loosen their hold upon Cymbeline himself. The lesser of them, Cloten, is drawn on in pursuit of Imogen until he trespasses upon the very outskirts of Paradise, where he is killed outright by the Spirit; and this indirectly kills his mother, who dies gradually of a fever brought on by frustration at his absence, by exasperation leading to despair. Thus the whole soul is finally set free from its bonds.

So far we have only considered the play from one angle, according to which Everyman is represented by the synthesis of Imogen and her father. But like *Antony and Cleopatra, Cymbeline* has a reversible symbolism: it is also the story of Posthumus Leonatus, and from this point of view it is he who stands for the soul and Imogen, the princess, who represents the Spirit. Imogen's transcendence is stressed throughout the play, by various characters in various ways. For Posthumus she is *a gift of the gods;* for one of the courtiers she is *divine Imogen* just as for Cassio Othello's wife is *divine Desdemona*; for Pisanio she is *more goddess-like than wife-life*; but perhaps the most significant of all, considering the wisdom of the speaker, is Belarius's exclamation when he first sees her (she is at that time disguised as a boy):

> By Jupiter, an angel! or if not
> An earthly paragon! Behold divineness
> No elder than a boy!   (III, 6)

The path of Posthumus Leonatus is a descent into Hell followed by an ascent of Purgatory. The sin of spiritual pride – manifested by his public boasting about Imogen – is brought to light, and brings with it its own retribution, a too easy loss of faith in Imogen, which breeds the sins of raging anger, treachery and, by intention, murder, for he treacherously seeks to lure Imogen to her death. It is only when the false news of her death comes to him that light dawns and his Purgatory begins. The change from the descent to the ascent is marked by his deciding to change sides in the battle and fight for Britain instead of Rome.

> I'll fight
> Against the part I come with; so I'll die
> For thee, O Imogen, even for whom my life
> is, every breath, a death.   (V, 1)

He helps Belarius and the two princes to rescue Cymbeline in the battle and to put the Romans to flight. Then, in despair at not having died, he gives himself up to the Britons as a Roman prisoner, hoping to find death that way, and is led off to prison. His eloquent prayer for Divine Mercy – a passage too little known on account of the language difficulties caused by its elliptical concentration – recalls Hamlet's *the readiness is all* and Edgar's *ripeness is all*. In Posthumus' case, 'ripeness' takes the form of having paid all debts, that is, of having expiated all sins or, in other words, of having passed through Purgatory in this life. He is altogether confident that the act of death will work the final purifying touch and win him the fullness of Divine Mercy, thus opening for him the door from the prison of Purgatory to the freedom of Paradise. His certainty is confirmed by the vision which he then has of blessed spirits from Elysium interceding with Jupiter on his behalf. It is in virtue of this that he can so flatly contradict the gaoler at the end of the same scene. The gist of their argument might be expressed as follows. The gaoler insists that death is a closed door and that no one knows for certain what lies on the other side of it. Posthumus maintains that death is an open door through which anyone who is prepared to open his eyes can see what lies beyond.

> *I tell thee, fellow, there are none want eyes to*
> *direct them the way I am going, but such as wink*
> *and will not use them.*   (v, 4)

The meaning already given to these words is the literal one in answer to the gaoler. But in the case of Posthumus this meaning coincides with a deeper one, for *the way I am going* is the path of the mysteries, 'the straitened way that leadeth unto life', and 'few are they that find it' because although it lies in front of everyone as the obvious course to take, most people turn a blind eye to it. The 'narrow gate' itself, however, is not reached by Posthumus until the final scene when, still thinking that he has killed Imogen, he learns that she is entirely innocent, and cries out:

> *O, give me cord, or knife, or poison,*
> *Some upright justicer! Thou, king, send out*
> *For torturers ingenious: it is I*
> *That all the abhorred things o' the earth amend*
> *By being worse than they.*

It is by virtue of his being *absolute for death*, like Claudio and Angelo in *Measure for Measure*, that he may be said to have 'died into life' just as much as those of Shakespeare's heroes and heroines who literally do die.

In *Antony and Cleopatra* the symbolism of Egypt and Rome is not reversible. For Cleopatra as well as for Antony Rome is this world, and at the end the choice for Cleopatra is between this world, represented by Rome and Caesar, and the next world represented by the dead Antony.[5] But in *Cymbeline* Britain and Rome have each a positive and a negative significance. Where Everyman is represented by Imogen and her father, the court of Britain represents this world just as it does in *King Lear*, and Kent's words

> *Freedom lies hence, and banishment is here*

might just as well be applied to Cymbeline's palace as to Lear's. One aspect of Cymbeline's corruption is that he has refused to pay tribute to Caesar; and there is also a special connection between Rome and Jupiter in virtue of *Jove's bird, the Roman eagle.* Moreover Caesar's ambassador Lucius, Rome's chief representative in this play, is extremely venerable. When advising Imogen to seek service with him, Pisanio says of him:

> *He's honourable,*
> *And, doubling that, most holy.*   (III, 4)

Considering the play from this point of view there is a certain identity between Rome and Belarius' cave inasmuch as both are spiritual centres with regard to which Cymbeline is at fault; and it is to be noted that Cloten, who is actually killed for his sacrilege of trespassing upon the precincts of the cave, has previously expressed his readiness to commit sacrilege with regard to the other sanctuary. In preparing to follow Imogen he says:

> *I will pursue her*
> *Even to Augustus' throne.*   (III, 5)

---

[5] It is true, however, that the presence of Antony in the next world,
> *a Roman by a Roman*
> *Valiantly vanquisht,*
adds as it were a certain 'prestige' to Rome; and although in the last scene Cleopatra says:
> *'Tis paltry to be Caesar;*
and although her own death and the deaths of her attendants are hastened on through the imperative need to escape being taken to Rome, of which she conjures up the most sordid pictures, she has none the less already said over Antony's dead body:
> *We'll bury him, and then, what's brave, what's noble,*
> *We'll do it after the high Roman fashion,*
> *And make death proud to take us;*
and the play ends on a note of grandeur and magnanimity from Caesar.

It is to be noted also that although the speeches expressing Britain's defiance of Rome have a patriotic ring about them and might seem in themselves to be positive, they are for the most part put by Shakespeare into the mouths of no more reputable characters than the Queen and her degenerate son.

On the other hand, from the point of view of the banished Posthumus, Britain, the abode of Imogen, is a Paradise. From this standpoint the faults of Cymbeline are not relevant. The soul, represented by Posthumus, is not yet worthy to be united with the Spirit, and has been justly banished. The celestial aspect of Britain is brought out strongly when the devilish Iachimo, who is a Roman, says that he feels the very air to be taking revenge upon him:

> *The heaviness and guilt within my bosom*
> *Takes off my manhood. I have belied a lady,*
> *The princess of this country, and the air on't*
> *Revengingly enfeebles me.*   (v, 2)

As we have seen, it is a milestone in Posthumus' spiritual journey when he discards his Italian clothes for the garb of a British peasant and decides to fight for Britain against Rome.

The two opposite points of view are reconciled at the end and merged into one standpoint from which both Britain and Rome are celestial. Cymbeline says:

> *Although the victor, we submit to Caesar*
> *And to the Roman empire,*[6] *promising*
> *To pay our wonted tribute, from the which*
> *We were dissuaded by our wicked queen;*
> *Whom heavens in justice on both her and hers*
> *Have laid most heavy hand.*

This reconciliation is the meaning of the soothsayer's vision:

> *The Roman eagle,*
> *From south to west on wing soaring aloft,*
> *Lessen'd herself and in the beams o' the sun*
> *So vanish'd: which foreshow'd our princely eagle,*

---

[6] To digress for the moment from Shakespeare's deepest meaning, and also from the literal meaning, is it possible to read into Cymbeline's somewhat unexpected submission a plea to the son of Mary Stuart to find some way of mending once more the breach between Britain and Rome?

> *The imperial Caesar, should again unite*
> *His favour with the radiant Cymbeline*
> *Which shines here in the west.*

Meantime, without our being able to say exactly how or when, the drama itself has been snatched up to a higher plane. The transition from earth to Heaven is not so clear-cut as at the end of *The Winter's Tale*, but the celestial effect is none the less overwhelmingly conveyed by the altogether unearthly piling up of happiness upon happiness – the sudden blissful perfect recovery of so much that had seemed to be irretrievably lost, the simultaneous realization of all the fullness of conjugal, filial and fraternal love. This celestial wealth of felicity finds perhaps above all its expression in Cymbeline's words:

> *See,*
> *Posthumus anchors upon Imogen;*
> *And she, like harmless lightning, throws her eye*
> *On him, her brothers, me, her master,[7] hitting*
> *Each object with a joy: the counterchange*
> *Is severally in all. Let's quit this ground,*
> *And smoke the temple with our sacrifices.*
> [To Belarius] *Thou art my brother, so we'll hold thee ever.*

---

[7] The Roman Lucius, whom she had served as page.

CHAPTER 11

THE WINTER'S TALE

Of all Shakespeare's plays the nearest parallel to *The Divine Comedy* is perhaps *The Winter's Tale*, though needless to say, even this cannot take us as far as Dante's epic does. Like the epic, however, it none the less falls into three distinct parts. For Leontes, as for Othello, Angelo and Posthumus, Hell and Purgatory are represented separately. The first part of *The Winter's Tale* deals with the discovery of the evil which until then had lurked hidden in the soul of Leontes. His behaviour in his first scene has something in common with Posthumus' boasting about Imogen. Both men are in possession of a secret treasure which in a sense they profane. Leontes' great fault is that he exploits the forces of the Spirit, represented by Hermione, for a purely trivial purpose. There is no reason why Polyxenes should stay any longer in Sicily and there are many reasons, so he tells us, why he should return to Bohemia. But Leontes squanders Hermione's irresistible power to make Polyxenes change his mind, and then even forgets himself so far as to say:

> *Hermione, my dearest, thou never spokest*
> *To better purpose.* (I, 2)

She takes him up on this point, and he admits that she had spoken to better purpose once before, namely when she had consented to marry him. But his admission cannot atone for the enormity of so monstrous a loss of sense of proportion. It is in fact no less than sacrilege, considering what his marriage means, although in his case as in the other cases we have seen, the union of soul and Spirit is as yet only virtual, the marriage signifying initiation rather than realization, for Leontes has not yet learnt to rate Hermione at her true worth.

To say, as is so often said, that the jealousy of Leontes is less convincing than that of Othello serves merely to confuse the issue. As we have already seen, it is impossible to represent all the different aspects of the truth in one play. Iago is a wonderful portrayal of the devil in all his hellishness; but at the price of such a portrait Shakespeare is scarcely able, in *Othello*, to convey the fact that the devil is inside the soul of fallen man as well as outside it. Leontes is Othello with Iago inside him. There is no outward personification of the devil in *The Winter's Tale*, or indeed of any evil, except for the knavery of Autolycus which has no direct bearing on the plot. The other characters stand round like guardian angels while Leontes plunges deeper and deeper into Hell. They know that he is not himself. What has already been said about Angelo in connection with Mariana's line:

> *They say best men are moulded out of faults*

applies equally well to Leontes. The lost psychic substance has first of all to be rediscovered and then purified and reintegrated, and there is or can be a dangerous moment between the discovery and the purification. Leontes has woken up dormant elements in his soul which have leapt upon him and overpowered him before he could subdue them. He is, as Camillo puts it, *in rebellion with himself*. But he has saved himself in advance by submitting the whole issue to the judgement of Apollo:

> *Yet for a greater confirmation,*
> *For in an act of this importance 'twere*
> *Most piteous to be wild, I have dispatch'd in post*
> *To sacred Delphos, to Apollo's temple,*
> *Cleomenes and Dion . . . now from the oracle*
> *They will bring all; whose spiritual counsel had,*
> *Shall stop or spur me.*   (II, 1)

Later we learn that Cleomenes and Dion have returned from Delphos with almost miraculous speed; and we are given a brief glimpse of them as they land in Sicily, quite overwhelmed by the blessedness of Apollo's temple, the solemn reverence of the priests, the unearthliness of the sacrifice, and the voice of the oracle which reduced the hearers to a feeling of nothingness. Shakespeare is clearly determined that God shall preside over his play, despite puritanical laws to the contrary!

Having disowned his new-born daughter and sent her to be left in some desert place where she is more likely to die than to live, Leontes

puts his wife Hermione on trial for adultery and treason. The descent
into Hell goes on, without any question of Purgatory, until finally
Hermione appeals to Apollo for justice. Cleomenes and Dion are called
into court and the statement of the oracle is read:

> *Hermione is chaste; Polyxenes blameless; Camillo a*
> *true subject; Leontes a jealous tyrant; his innocent*
> *babe truly begotten; and the king shall live without*
> *an heir, if that which is lost be not found.*   (III, 2)

The oracle precipitates Leontes to the nethermost depth of Hell and
he cries out:

> *There is not truth at all i' the oracle,*
> *The session shall proceed; this is mere falsehood.*

thus bringing to light the greatest of all evils, impiety against Heaven.
Immediate retribution follows: unknown to any of those present, the
King's son is dead and the King is in fact *without an heir* except for *that
which is lost*, the baby daughter whom he has cast out. No sooner has
Leontes uttered his blasphemy than a servant enters, announcing the
death of the Prince. This one terrible blow shatters in an instant all the
rebellion in Leontes' soul. We have seen that in *Othello*, when Emilia
suddenly proves beyond doubt Desdemona's innocence and Iago's
guilt, the whole of the Moor's dark descent into Hell is immediately lit
up in retrospect. Symbolically, that moment is the exact equivalent of
the *Fiat lux* brought about by the oracle in *The Winter's Tale*. At the news
of his son's death, the scales fall from Leontes' eyes, and seeing exactly
what has happened, he is all repentance. Meantime his wife has fainted
and is carried off; and then the news is brought that she, too, is dead.

The Purgatory of Leontes takes place in the interval of the sixteen
years which elapse between this act and the next. But although it is not
represented on the stage, Shakespeare gives us a wonderful glimpse, at
its outset, of the immensity of the task in all its apparent hopelessness,
and of the soul's contrition which makes all things possible. Paulina says
to Leontes:

> *A thousand knees*
> *Ten thousand years together, naked, fasting,*
> *Upon a barren mountain, and still winter*
> *In storm perpetual, could not move the gods*
> *To look that way thou wert.*

Leontes replies:

> Go on, go on;
> Thou canst not speak too much; I have deserv'd
> All tongues to talk their bitterest.

After he has said at the end of the scene

> Come, lead me to these sorrows,

we do not see him again until the sixteen years have passed.

This undisguised miracle play is intensified in its effect upon us by the symbolism of death and birth combined with that of winter and spring. It is Leontes' son, the young Prince Mamillius, who dies; and it is he who tells the winter's tale, the story of Hell and Purgatory. When asked by Hermione to tell her a *merry* tale he says:

> A sad tale's best for winter.   (II, 1)

He then puts his mouth close to his mother's ear to whisper to her his 'tale about the man who dwelt by a churchyard', and just at that moment the raging Leontes rushes in, and sets in motion the train of sorrowful events. The last of these is that when Perdita, the new-born daughter of Leontes, has been left in a desert place in Bohemia, Antigonus who left her there is killed by a bear and the crew of his boat are shipwrecked. These deaths are witnessed by the son of a shepherd; meantime Perdita has been found by the shepherd himself, who says to his son:

> Thou mettest with things dying, I with things new-born.
>   (III, 3)

This brings a new note into the play, and identifies Perdita with birth, just as her brother was identified with death; and when next we see her, after sixteen years, she is dressed as Flora, the Goddess of Spring. This sheep-shearing festival scene, like the whole of the second part of the play, takes place in late summer, which is the season that Leontes has now reached in life. But Shakespeare overstamps this season with the seal of spring in the characters of Perdita and Florizel; when they decide to elope to Sicily, we know that with their coming the tale of winter will end for Leontes, and the tale of spring will begin.

This is confirmed by the opening speech of the next scene, which has already been quoted in an earlier chapter. We are once more with Leontes in Sicily, and Cleomenes says to him:

> *Sir, you have done enough, and have performed*
> *A saint-like sorrow; no fault could you make*
> *which you have not redeem'd; indeed, paid down*
> *More penitence than done trespass; at the last*
> *Do as the heavens have done, forget your evil;*
> *With them forgive yourself.*   (v, 1)

These words tell us that we are now at the point beyond which the plays of the middle period do not go.

A gentleman comes in to announce the arrival of Florizel, Prince of Bohemia, accompanied by his princess, of whom it is said:

> *Women will love her, that she is a woman*
> *More worth than any man; men, that she is*
> *The rarest of all women.*

Paulina says:

> *Had our prince –*
> *Jewel of children – seen this hour, he had pair'd*
> *Well with this lord: there was not full a month*
> *Between their birth.*

This indicates that Florizel is to replace the dead Prince Mamillius. He and Perdita together, like Cymbeline's two sons, thus represent the 'immortality' of primordial man which was lost and has now been found again.

Leontes is now on the very threshold of the Earthly Paradise, and the sight of Florizel and Perdita is as a vision of that Paradise. The entry of the Prince and Princess can be quite overwhelming, provided that those who play their parts are adequate, and provided that there is the right kind of music (we will come back to this question later), continuing long enough, after their entry, to enable them to 'beget wonder' in Leontes and his court, and also in the audience, before Leontes says to them:

> *I lost a couple, that 'twixt heaven and earth*
> *Might thus have stood begetting wonder as*
> *You, gracious couple, do;*

and later:

> *Welcome hither,*
> *As is the spring to the earth.*

The vision of Paradise fades for the moment, but only to give place to something more than a vision, for in the next scene we are told of his discovery that Perdita is his daughter, and thus he regains *that which was lost*.

The final scene takes us further. The Earthly Paradise is the gateway to the Heavenly Paradise, which is the theme of the third part of Dante's epic; and although according to the literal meaning of *The Winter's Tale* Hermione never really died at all, but has remained hidden for sixteen years, the audience, for once, have not been taken into the secret. They, like Leontes, are sure that she is dead and in Heaven. Her appearance in the last scene has therefore the implicit effect of raising that scene to a celestial plane and of making us certain that husband and wife will, quite literally, 'live together happily ever afterwards'.

CHAPTER 12

THE TEMPEST

The Tempest is by general consent Shakespeare's last complete play. We have already seen something of how it is anticipated by both *A Midsummer Night's Dream* and *Measure for Measure*. But the most immediately obvious parallel to *The Tempest* is *As You Like It*. In both the reigning duke is driven out of his duchy by a usurping brother; the plot of each turns round the love story of the rightful duke's daughter who has also been exiled; in each the usurping brother finally repents and the rightful duke gains once more possession of his duchy: and the most striking resemblance of all is that each takes place in a setting which is beyond – and above – the confines of civilization.

The forest of Arden represents the Golden Age. The banished duke and his followers are said to *fleet the time carelessly, as they did in the golden world*. We are transported back to an age when man still lived as it were in the neighbourhood of the lost Paradise.

> Here feel we but the penalty of Adam,
> The season's difference . . .
> And this our life exempt from public haunts
> Finds tongues in trees, books in the running brooks,
> Sermons in stones, and good in everything.
> I would not change it.   (II, 1)

says the Duke. The enchanted island of *The Tempest* also transcends the rest of the world. Like the forest of the earlier play it is near to Heaven and therefore the ideal setting for the love that symbolizes the reunion of the celestial with the terrestrial. At the end of *As You Like It*, Rosalind is led on by Hymen who says:

> *Good Duke receive thy daughter:*
> *Hymen from heaven brought her.*

And in *The Tempest*, as we have already seen, the 'marriage' of Heaven
and earth actually takes place in the persons of Juno and Ceres, who are
brought together by Iris, the celestial rainbow messenger, to attend the
betrothal of Miranda and Ferdinand.

   In addition to the already mentioned resemblance between *The
Tempest* and *Measure for Measure*, it may be noted that if Prospero is
banished from Milan, the Duke is also banished – self banished – from
Vienna; and if the Duke secretly remains in Vienna to observe what
happens in his supposed absence, Prospero keeps Milan under his
observation by transporting it, together with Naples from which it is
symbolically inseparable, to his island. Naples and Milan, like Vienna,
are this world. In a sense the whole world is on board the boat; and at the
centre of that world stands Alonso, the King of Naples, with his son
Ferdinand. After appearing briefly in the scene of the shipwreck which
opens the play, they retire below and we do not see them again on deck,
though we are made to feel their presence. Gonzalo says:

> *The king and prince at prayers! Let's assist them,*
> *For our case is as theirs.*

This remark is more significant than it might appear, for it is calculated
to find an echo in the souls of the audience. They likewise are on board
the boat of this world, which the tempest has revealed in its true light as
the highly precarious and dangerous place that in fact it is. We may also
note that the speaker of these words is defined in the *dramatis personae* as
'An honest old Counsellor', and throughout the play he is something of
a prolongation of Prospero himself. The actor who plays his part would
be justified in addressing this speech to everyone, off stage as well as on,
for the best of the audience, whether they know it or not, have come to
the theatre to identify themselves with the two men who are *at prayers*,
and of whom anyone with a true sense of reality can and must say:

> *Let's assist them,*
> *For our case is as theirs.*

   The King and Prince in this play, like the King and Princess in
Cymbeline, together represent the human soul which is on its way
through purification to sanctification. Hell is not portrayed, except in
retrospect; the powers of evil are present, but they are already under

control. Prospero's treacherous brother Antonio, the usurping Duke of Milan, has much in common with Claudius in *Hamlet*. It was Antonio who had contrived to bring about the exile of the Spirit by seducing the soul, in the person of the King of Naples, into an unholy alliance.

The greater part of Purgatory is concentrated in the tempest at the opening of the play. The enchanted island itself is no less than a setting for the sacred precinct of Prospero's cell, which may be said to transcend Purgatory. By extension the rest of the island is also a sanctuary; even Caliban is aware of its blessedness:

> Be not afear'd; the isle is full of noises,
> Sounds and sweet airs, that give delight and hurt not
> Sometimes a thousand twangling instruments
> Will hum about mine ears; and sometimes voices,
> That if I then had waked after long sleep,
> Will make me sleep again: and then, in dreaming,
> The clouds methought would open, and show riches
> Ready to drop upon me; that, when I waked,
> I cried to dream again.   (III, 2)

Alonso and Ferdinand reach the island separately. It must be remembered that in the King-Prince Everyman of this play, as in the pair Cymbeline-Imogen, it is the parent who personifies the old and fallen soul, and the child who is virtually the new perfect soul which is waiting to be delivered.[1] That moment has now come, inasmuch as the son is certain his father is dead. Despite the considerable difference of details between the Prince of *The Tempest* and the Prince of *Henry IV* Ferdinand is now in a situation which recalls the scene where Prince Henry places the crown on his own head, believing himself to be already King. The parallel is all the stronger in that both Princes are at the outskirts of Paradise, for Prince Henry crowns himself at the threshold of the Jerusalem Chamber.[2] Symbolically, the belief of each that he is King may be said to be equivalent to the actuality of kingship; and true kingship signifies, as we have seen,[3] man's primal state, fallen man being a usurper to the throne of earth. But in The Tempest, unlike the earlier play, the regenerated perfection of the Prince is made more clearly implicit at this point not only by Ariel's confirmation of the King's death

[1] See p.103.
[2] See p.26.
[3] p.25

and burial *full fathom five*, but also and above all by the use of Hermetic symbolism.

The boat, apparently on fire when Ferdinand left it – *all afire with me*, as Ariel says – is the funeral pyre, the Athanor of the alchemists. One might at first be surprised that Shakespeare does not pursue this fiery theme exclusively, and that he should speak of the sacrificial vessel not as a pyre but as a *wreck*, and of the alchemical transmutations themselves not as a fire-change but as a *sea-change*. However, quite apart from the fact that fire is not, throughout this play, the dominant element in the consciousness of the audience, water is here a technical necessity, for it represents the first of the two terms of the great formula *solve et coagula*, and it is none other than the Quicksilver which has to be penetrated by the fire of Sulphur. 'Through the union of opposites the soul becomes "fluid fire" and "fiery water".'[4] The tempest itself, after which the play is named, is the alchemical 'work', and Ariel assures Prospero that it was effectively an interpenetration of fire and water:

> *the fire and cracks*
> *Of sulphurous roaring the most mighty Neptune*
> *Seem to besiege, and make his bold waves tremble.*   (I, 2)

Prospero is here the Master Alchemist, and the result of his 'work' is the Prince himself, who later speaks of his future father-in-law as being the one *of whom I have received a second life* (V, 1). Ferdinand may thus be considered as the new-born Phoenix which rises from the flames and from the waves.

It is as such that he now enters upon us, his natural beauty enhanced by the beauty of the music and of his wonderment at it, as well as by the beauty of the words he speaks, and of the words that Ariel then sings:

> *Where should this music be? i'th'air or th'earth?*
> *It sounds no more: and, sure, it waits upon*
> *Some god o'th'island. Sitting on a bank,*
> *Weeping again the king my father's wreck,*
> *This music crept by me upon the waters,*
> *Allaying both their fury and my passion*[5]
> *With its sweet air: thence I have follow'd it,*
> *Or it hath drawn me rather. But 'tis gone.*
> *No, it begins again.*

---

[4] Titus Burckhardt, *Alchemy*, p.74.
[5] Suffering.

Ariel sings:

> *Full fathom five thy father lies;*
> *Of his bones are coral made;*
> *Those are pearls which were his eyes:*
> *Nothing of him that doth fade,*
> *But doth suffer a sea-change*
> *Into something rich and strange.*   (I, 2)

Wonderment is an essential characteristic of primordial man inasmuch as wondrousness is an essential quality of Paradise which is his home. The heroine of this play has not been named at random; and when Ferdinand first sees her, thinking she must be a goddess in whose service the music is played, he addresses her, even before he knows her name:

> *O you wonder!;*

and later he is to say, this time with reference to Prospero:

> *Let me live here ever;*
> *So rare a wonder'd*[6]*father and a wise*
> *Makes this place Paradise.*   (IV, 1)

Miranda, the Marvellous, is also necessarily the marvelling. When Ferdinand enters she is asleep, but she gradually awakens during Ariel's song, which may be said to prepare her for a vision of *something rich and strange.*[7] The song itself is directly concerned with King Alonso, but also points to the Prince. To affirm the death of the old soul is to herald the birth of the new perfect soul; and it is Ferdinand himself who, as we have seen, embodies the result of the *sea-change* which is Ariel's theme. Shortly after the music ends, or perhaps[8] while the *burthen* or undersong still continues as a soft accompaniment to the spoken word, her father bids her open her eyes, to see what she can see; and it is as with the wonderment of Eve at her first sight of Adam that she sets eyes on the Prince, never before having seen a man other than her father:

> *I might well call him*
> *A thing divine; for nothing natural*
> *I ever saw so noble.*

---

[6] Possessed of wonders, able to work wonders.
[7] This word is much nearer to 'wonderful' in Shakespeare's use of it than in ours.
[8] According to the production.

Rich and strange: these two epithets strike the key-note of this scene, and indeed of the play as a whole. Both reoccur at the climax, when Prospero gives Miranda to Ferdinand and says, with regard to the ordeal which he has imposed upon him:

> *All thy vexations*
> *Were but my trials of thy love, and thou*
> *Hast strangely[9] stood the test: here, afore Heaven,*
> *I ratify this my rich gift. O Ferdinand.*
> *Do not smile at me that I boast her off,*
> *For thou shalt find she will outstrip all praise,*
> *And make it halt behind her.*   (IV, 1)

If we draw a comparison between Shakespeare's first great drama of love and this his last, it goes without saying that the essential in both is the factor of love itself, the mutual human attraction at its highest degree in virtue of each consort being the other's lost and longed for half.[10] But in *Romeo and Juliet* the magnitude of the love is stressed by being measured out against the formidable strength of the adverse circumstances over which, unshakeable and invincible, it triumphs. In *The Tempest* on the other hand the circumstances are altogether favourable; unlike their less fortunate predecessors, Ferdinand and Miranda have the stars on their side. Their union is expressly blessed, not only by Heaven, Juno, but also by Earth, Ceres. There is every outward or secondary reason why they should be married, whereas the love of Romeo and Juliet is in sharp conflict with its earthly setting. The union of these star-crossed lovers of old Verona is a metacosmic or celestial necessity in tragic collision with a cosmic impossibility. The ultimate triumph of Heaven is marked by their burial side by side and their statues of pure gold. The union of Ferdinand and Miranda is likewise a marriage that has been made in Heaven, while being at the same time a cosmic necessity. Their wedding will be, moreover, the wedding of two 'worlds', Milan and Naples; nor is this its only macrocosmic significance, for there is also one of a deeper and a more universal order: the irresistibility of each lover for the other takes on an added vastness from the fact that Ferdinand is for Miranda quite literally the one and only man, whereas she is for him, as he tells her expressly, the sum of feminine virtue.

These remarks are not intended to exalt their love over that of Romeo

---

[9] Wonderfully.
[10] See p.45.

and Juliet, which is clearly unsurpassable – to the point of being almost proverbial. As such, it stands in no danger of being underestimated. But the love of Ferdinand and Miranda must also be allowed its own unique and unsurpassable quality – a quality which is in a sense the measure of the greatness of the masterpiece to which it belongs. To praise *The Tempest* is to praise its love scenes, which are essential to it; and the following exclamation of Prospero, whole-heartedly echoed by the audience, may be said to sum up the play:

> *Fair encounter*
> *Of two most rare affections!* (III, 1)

If it be asked which of the lovers represents the Spirit and which the soul, the answer is clearly that the symbolism is reversible, as in *Romeo and Juliet, Antony and Cleopatra*, and other plays. Miranda is Prospero's daughter; and the significance of the place of her upbringing, far from the corruption of the world, has already been mentioned in this very context.[11] We must not forget, however, that at the first meeting of these lovers, each thinks that the other is divine; and Miranda's attitude of worship is altogether in line with the way in which, by Prospero's contriving, she has her first 'vision' of the Prince. Moreover, once her father has entrusted her to him, this future King will take, insofar as she is concerned, the place of Prospero. On the one hand, then, it may be said that Prospero stands for the Spirit-Intellect, and that Miranda is an extension of him, just as Perdita is an extension of Hermione, who, like Desdemona and Cordelia, is the 'pearl of great price' which was wantonly thrown away. On the other hand Miranda is Prospero's disciple who, from her earliest years, has followed the path of his guidance, a path of which the ultimate goal is the illustrious marriage that he has planned for her. From this point of view, which takes into consideration also the symbolism of rank, it is the future King of Naples who represents the Spirit and Miranda the soul.

We will return to this second relationship later. But as regards King Alonso, it is the first which is relevant, for to repeat in other terms what has already been said, he represents the 'lead' of the soul, the base metal in which Ferdinand is the potential 'gold'. 'According to the famous Moslem mystic Muhyi'd-Dīn ibn 'Arabī, gold corresponds to the sound and original condition of the soul which freely and without distortion reflects the Divine Spirit in its essence, whereas lead corresponds to its

[11] pp.101-102

"sick", distorted, and "dead" condition, which no longer reflects the Spirit. The true essence of lead is gold. Each base metal represents a break in the equilibrium which gold alone exhibits. In order to free the soul from its coagulation and paralysis, its essential form and its *materia*[12] must be dissolved out of their crude and one-sided combination. It is as if spirit[13] and soul had to be separated from one another, in order, after their "divorce", to become "married" again. The amorphous *materia* is burnt, dissolved, and purified, in order finally to be "coagulated" anew.'[14] The King and the Prince, like Cymbeline and Imogen, represent precisely the 'crude and one-sided combination' that is mentioned here – one-sided because in both cases it is the base metal which has the sovereign power; and the above passage shows that the temporary separation of Ferdinand and Alonso is alchemically necessary. Highly significant in this respect is the question which, at his first sight of Miranda, the father puts to his son:

> Is she the goddess that hath sever'd us,
> And brought us thus together?   (v, 1)

Miranda is here a prolongation of the Master Alchemist, upon whom Alonso, like Ferdinand, depends entirely for his spiritual regeneration. In passing through the Athanor of the tempest, he dies the death of believing that his son is dead; and the end of his Purgatory is marked by his complete repentance, after Ariel, at Prospero's command, has caused him to be penetrated through and through by a sense of his guilt. Alonso says:

> O, it is monstrous, monstrous!
> Methought the billows spoke and told me of it;
> The winds did sing it to me; and the thunder,
> That deep and dreadful organ-pipe, pronounced
> The name of Prosper: it did bass my trespass.
> Therefore my son i'th'ooze is bedded; and

[12] Its 'condition of base metal, especially lead which in its obscurity and heaviness resembles crude mass' (Titus Buckhardt, *op. cit.*, p.72).

[13] Spelled without a capital, spirit here means the essential 'gold' in the soul in virtue of which it is a prolongation or reflection of the Spirit in the strict sense. In other words, that is, in the terms of the persons of this play, if 'spirit and soul', as used above, are respectively Ferdinand and Alonso, the soul in its full and normal significance must be named Ferdinand-Alonso, with Prospero-Miranda as Spirit.

[14] *Ibid.*, pp.72-3.

> *I'll seek him deeper than e'er plummet sounded,*
> *And with him there lie mudded.*   (III, 3)

Later, when he meets Prospero, still thinking that his son is dead and
thinking also that Prospero has lost his daughter, his complete sincerity
is not to be doubted when he says:

> *O heavens, that they were living both in Naples,*
> *The king and queen there! that they were, I wish*
> *Myself were mudded in that oozy bed*
> *Where my son lies.*   (V, 1)

It is only when Alonso's repentance is assured that Ferdinand, for his
part, comes to the end of his ordeal of carrying logs, and Prospero
consents to his marriage with Miranda. When Prospero finally reveals
the betrothed couple to Alonso, this King may be said to have reached
exactly the same point that is reached by the repentant and purified King
in *The Winter's Tale* when Perdita and Florizel come to his court.

There is no character in *The Tempest* to correspond to Hermione.
Instead, a stress is laid on the difference between betrothal and
marriage. The Earthly Paradise is not the complete union of soul and
Spirit but the leaning down as it were of Spirit to soul, of Heaven to
earth. In the Earthly Paradise, symbolized here by the betrothal of
Ferdinand and Miranda, Everyman has reached the fullness of earthly
possibility. It is therefore at this point that Prospero prepares Ferdinand
and Miranda for the Greater Mysteries of the Celestial Paradise by
telling them that all the glories of earthly life are nothing more than a
dream:

> *Our revels now are ended. These our actors,*
> *As I foretold you, were all spirits, and*
> *Are melted into air, into thin air:*
> *And like the baseless fabric of this vision,*
> *The cloud-capp'd towers, the gorgeous palaces,*
> *The solemn temples, the great globe itself,*
> *Yea, all which it inherit, shall dissolve,*
> *And, like this insubstantial pageant faded,*
> *Leave not a wrack behind. We are such stuff*
> *As dreams are made on; and our little life*
> *Is rounded with a sleep.*   (IV, 1)

The Celestial Paradise is not represented in *The Tempest*, as it is in *The*

Winter's Tale, but the whole play reciprocates its leaning down by reaching up towards it, that is, towards the final marriage of the lovers.

As in *Cymbeline*, the hierarchic precedence of places is reversible as well as that of the lovers. The enchanted island, like the cave of Belarius, transcends the corrupt world of civilization; but that world will no longer be the same now that its inhabitants, and in particular its rulers, have been purified. At the end of *The Tempest* Milan and Naples take on a purely positive significance as things which were lost and are regained. The two points of view, as regards place and person, are intertwined in the last scene. For King Alonso, as for his son, Miranda is divine; for her, on the other hand, her future kingdom, personified by the Neopolitan visitors to the island, is the object to be marvelled at:

> *O, wonder!*
> *How many goodly creatures are there here!*
> *How beauteous mankind is! O brave new world,*
> *That has such people in't!*

Gonzalo has already been quoted as saying in the first scene:

> *The king and prince at prayers! let's assist them,*
> *For our case is as theirs.*

Equally chracteristic of his function in the play is his final summing up in the last scene, for here also he spreads wide the 'net' as if to include as many persons as possible in the blessing of the alchemical work:

> *Was Milan thrust from Milan, that his issue*
> *Should become kings of Naples? O, rejoice*
> *Beyond a common joy! and set it down*
> *With gold on lasting pillars; in one voyage*
> *Did Claribel her husband find at Tunis,*
> *And Ferdinand, her brother, found a wife*
> *Where he himself was lost, Prospero his dukedom*
> *In a poor isle, and all of us ourselves*
> *When no man was his own.*

The transcendent significance of the play and its final issue is here doubly affirmed by the two imperatives *Rejoice beyond a common joy* and *Set it down with gold*. The latter is also clearly an alchemical reference; and in connection with the closing words of this speech we may repeat the already quoted dictum, 'The true essence of lead is gold', in the sense that only primordial man knows and is his true self, fallen man having 'lost' his first nature, beneath the rubble of 'second nature' symbolized by lead.

'Let me know myself, Lord, and I shall know Thee', said St Augustine; and it may be recalled here that the Duke in *Measure for Measure* – a character very relevant to *The Tempest* – is defined as *One that, above all other strifes, contended especially to know himself.*[15] To find and know one's true self is the end of the Lesser Mysteries; but as the above saying of St Augustine teaches us, this is a stage on the way to a higher knowledge. What Gonzalo says may thus be taken as pointing also, implicitly and in aspiration, to knowledge of the Real Self in whose image the human self is made; nor would this be out of keeping with the play as a whole which reaches up towards these Greater Mysteries, that is, towards the marriage beyond the betrothal.

The play may also be said to reach up towards them in another sense. Again and again in his plays Shakespeare has likened this life either to the part played by an actor on the stage, or to a shadow, or to a dream. Now to speak of a play or any kind of fiction necessarily means that as a term of comparison one has in mind something which may be called 'real life'; to be continually likening things to shadows suggests a longing for the substance; and to dismiss everything that we experience and possess as a mere dream betrays a nostalgia for the state of being awake. But in order to reach that state of waking, that is, the Paradise of seeing 'face to face' and not 'as in a glass darkly', it is necessary to pass through that sleep which is the surrounding wall of the dream-world in which we live; and it is clearly in view of that sleep as a gate – for in itself it is not worth meditating on – that Shakespeare, about to give up his art and retire to Stratford, makes Prospero say, when about to give up *his* art and retire to Milan:

Every third thought shall be my grave.

---

[15] III, 2. Both these quotations are given by Whitall Perry in the section on 'Know Thyself' (pp.859-868) of his monumental *Treasury of Traditional Wisdom* (Perennial Books), and the reader will find there a wealth of other formulations of this universal rule, many of them being from Hermetic, Pythagorean, Platonic, Christian and other sources within the orbit of Shakespeare.

CHAPTER 13

NOTES ON PERFORMANCE AND PRODUCTION

How can actors and producers best do justice to the deeper meaning of Shakespeare's plays? A general answer to this question is: by being as faithful as possible to the literal meaning. Take care of that, and the deeper meaning will take care of itself. But to be true to the letter is less easy and more exacting than it may sound, for Shakespeare's maturer plays, even as regards their literal meaning, centre round human perfection, if not already achieved at any rate in the making – a perfection that is absolute and unsurpassable:

> *A combination and a form indeed*
> *Where every god did seem to set his seal*
> *To give the world assurance of a man.*

Shakespeare has in view a universal norm, a coin which would remain current even as far East as feudal Japan, and as far West as the Red Indians of North America – a complex but not complicated psychic substance made up of marvellously rich elements which are closely woven into a total effect of unity, simplicity and unfathomable depth; and this ideal spells great danger to an actor, for it cannot fail to measure out his capacities to their very fullest extent.

In *Hamlet*, for example, the actor may be said to have failed in his part if in the last scene the audience does not assent whole-heartedly to Horatio's admiring exclamation:

> *Why, what a king is this!*

and to Fortinbras' last words over the Prince's dead body:

He was likely, had he been put on,
To have proved most royally.

Similarly, to take another example, the actor of the part of Antony
cannot afford to forget during his performance that at the end, when
Antony's men find him dying, they are to say:

The star is fallen.
And time is at his period.[1]   (IV, 14)

and that Cleopatra is to say, when he actually dies:

There is nothing left remarkable
Beneath the visiting moon.   (IV, 15)

But if, as a loophole of escape, from a greatness hard to portray, the
actor seizes on the word 'dotage' so often applied to Antony by
Cleopatra's enemies, and if he sets out to portray a man who, however
great he may have been, is now psychically dilapidated, then the whole
significance of the play will be seriously impaired. No actor would,
however, admit, even to himself, that for fear of putting on a garment
that was too big for him, he was cutting down the garment to fit his own
size. The conscious motive for side-tracking is usually the desire to be
thought original or 'up to date'. However that may be, an actor may well
stand in fear of a central Shakespearean part; and whatever the motive,
it happens all too often that the main issue, which is one of sincerity and
depth, is avoided, and as a miserable 'compensation' all sorts of
psychological subtleties, quite unwarranted by the text, are invented.

   To illustrate this question still further let us take an example from a
play that so far has been mentioned no more than by name; and since the
plays written before *Hamlet* have scarcely come within the scope of this
book except incidentally, it must be admitted here and now, while
leaving the all-important question of total effect to be considered in the
next chapter, that if we were to choose out the greatest single scenes
from Shakespeare, or the greatest single moments, not a few of these
would be found to come from the earlier plays. One such moment is in
Twelfth Night. But if the part of Olivia be made comic through
affection – as it sometimes is – this moment will be sadly diminished, if
not reduced to nothing. As regards her love for Cesario, that is, for the
disguised Viola – who, it must be remembered, is consciously imitating

[1] Time has reached its final phase.

her twin brother Sebastian – it is essential that it should be portrayed with all the depth and sincerity that an actress can muster. It must be intense enough to compel the audience to echo in thought Viola's 'alas!' when she says:

> As I am a woman, – now, alas the day! –
> What thriftless sighs shall poor Olivia breathe!
> O Time, thou must untangle this, not I;
> It is too hard a knot for me t'untie.   (II, 2)

It is clear that Shakespeare intended the audience to share this sentiment; for only if their feelings are properly roused can the 'knot's' sudden and blissful 'untanglement' makes its full impact, when Olivia comes running out of the house to protect her beloved Cesario – as she thinks – from her uncle, and finds herself face to face with Sebastian for the first time. Several factors contribute to the strength of that impact, and not the least of these is its unexpectedness. So well contrived is it that however often we have seen the play before, it tends to come as something of a shock, partly because our attention is absorbed by the comic effect of the mistaken identity on Sir Toby and Sir Andrew and we are expecting more comic effects rather than a profoundly serious one. But by far the chief factor is the audience's deep concern for Olivia's happiness, and this can only be assured if they take her and her love altogether seriously. Shakespeare has already paved the way for them to do this by making the Duke say, in the first scene, in reference to her long mourning for her dead brother:

> O, she that hath a heart of that fine frame
> To pay this debt of love but to a brother,
> How will she love, when the rich golden shaft
> Hath killed the flock of all affections else
> That live in her!

Sebastian is no less than the lost half, the perfect complement, which Olivia has always, perhaps unconsciously, been yearning to recover. She is therefore not so very much mistaken when she falls in love with the disguised Viola, for in view of the irresistible mutual attraction which has always existed virtually between herself and Sebastian it is not unnatural that for want of ever having seen him she should feel a foretaste of that love on seeing his disguised twin sister, enough even to prefer her to all the world. From the abnormality of this strange and somewhat puzzling situation Shakespeare snatches something of the abnormality of miracle. Viola has already become for the audience, as far as Olivia is concerned, a symbol of all that the soul most deeply desires. Sebastian is therefore something more than a symbol. In him the shadow has given place to the substance. It is as if he had dropped straight from Heaven; and it is in the 'opening of Heaven' that there lies the secret of this moment's extraordinary power.

The effect of this first meeting between Olivia and Sebastian can be immeasurably deepened by the accompaniment of music.[2] This brings us from the question of acting to that of production, though the two things necessarily overlap, since in most modern productions the director is mainly responsible for the interpretation of the parts.

Despite what some may say, it is very conceivable that Shakespeare would have welcomed many of the facilities of the modern theatre, at any rate in principle. He might well have been glad to exploit some of the scenic effects which can be obtained now and could not then. He would almost certainly have preferred not to have his medieval kings and queens all dressed as Elizabethans as they were in his own productions. But the wider range of possibilities has also its drawbacks, for it opens the door to many blunders which would have been out of the question in Shakespeare's own day. There might seem to be a certain logic in the argument that since Shakespeare produced his plays in the sort of clothes that were worn by his audience why should we not do the same? Might it not make the audience feel more 'at home'? But apart from the fact that the audience do not go to Shakespeare in order to be made to feel 'at home' – or rather they go in order to be made to feel at home in quite a different way – Shakespeare in modern dress does not make them feel at home in any sense at all. The utter disparity between Shakespearean verse and twentieth century fashion is bound to create a feeling of uneasiness even in the least critical members of an audience. Whatever the limitations of early Jacobean and late Elizabethan dress may be, it at least belongs to the tail-end of a tradition which was based on the conception of man as the representative of God on earth. In those days garments were still conceived of as a means of enhancing the dignity and beauty of man's body just as verse and poetic imagery are a means of enhancing the dignity and beauty of man's speech. But modern dress, which to say the least has no such pretensions, cannot possibly

---

[2] This can be achieved most successfully – and most naturally – if Olivia's musicians are playing indoors, and the music suddenly becomes louder when she runs out.

join forces with the splendours of Shakespeare's language.[3] It can only fight against that splendour, fatally diminishing its impact upon us.

We are taking here an extreme case. Fortunately productions of Shakespeare in modern dress are comparatively rare. But the objections to them apply also, in a lesser degree, to any attempts to give the plays a modern slant. The shoe simply cannot be made to fit, and when we are forced to wear it, it hurts. If Shakespeare was 'not of an age but for all time' this does not mean that his plays can be twisted into line with the particular limitations of each successive age, least of all our own age which on the surface is so very remote from his ideals. If he was 'for all time' and therefore of our age also, this is because he was an intellectual in the ancient sense of the word, with his eye on the universal, and because the universal is by definition always present, however little it may be in evidence. It was in virtue of his intellectuality that Shakespeare, unlike his contemporary dramatists, was able to escape from the prison of his own age into the universal world of Plato and St Augustine. What therefore can be more perverse than to seek to imprison him in the particular limitations of our own age? Besides, a Shakespeare audience is composed of people who have chosen to come of their own free will, and who could have gone, if they had wanted, to a modern play instead. They are certainly not present because they are men and women of the twentieth century but because they are men and women; and it would not perhaps be far wrong to say that even if for the most part they are not fully conscious of it, they are present because they are men and women who have in them something which is in danger of being starved to death by the twentieth century.

However that may be, there can be no doubt that the ideal in production is that the text should make as strong an impact as possible upon the audience. This is what the audience wants above all. And what director would dare to admit that this is not his aim? But there can be no strength without unity; and how seldom it is today that a director succeeds in uniting all the different elements in his production. How often, when the dresses are admirable or at least adequate, their effect upon us is ruined by a bleak semi-surrealist setting. And even when the eye is satisfied in every respect, and when if the ear were correspondingly

---

[3] Neither can nineteenth-century dress, for the same reason. Nor, for different reasons, can eighteenth-century dress, for though the age of white wigs would certainly have claimed that its dress enhanced the dignity of man's body, the artificiality and effeteness of its style is so alien to the spirit of Shakespeare that here again we should have the weakness of discord rather than the strength of concord.

satisfied the audience would be taken by storm, how seldom it is that we are not given some quite mediocre utterly unmoving sounds specially composed for the occasion.

When it was suggested to one of our leading directors of Shakespeare that he should make more use of Elizabethan music, he objected that this would oblige him to dress the actors like Elizabethans, which would give the production an aspect of 'quaintness'. It cannot be denied that there is something fantastic about Elizabethan dress which is not to be found in any dress that preceded it. By comparison, Tudor dress, to take the nearest example, has nothing of the 'quaintness' and limitedness – non-universality one might say – of the costume in which Shakespeare's plays were first acted. It was no doubt the defect of non-universality that the director in question was driving at. But Elizabethan music is not to be classed with all the other features of its period. We have been educated to think of the past, at any rate as regards Europe, century by century. But not all centuries are equally isolated. The thirteenth, fourteenth and fifteenth centuries for example have each their own special characteristics which distinguish them from one another, but these differences are made relatively insignificant by being submerged beneath a medieval sameness inasmuch as this period all belongs to the Christian civilization, that is, the theocratic civilization which has its roots in Christianity and is dominated by it. On the other hand the centuries from the seventeenth onwards are merely distinct from each other, for in their case there is no positive unifying factor. As to the transitional sixteenth century, the Middle Ages were not quite over in England, even as late as Shakespeare's day. The mere fact that a thing was Elizabethan or even early Jacobean leaves therefore unanswered the more important question as to whether or not it belongs to the Christian civilization. Elizabethan dress certainly does not, but Shakespeare's plays do, and so also does much Elizabethan music, and even much early Jacobean music. Whatever features of ancient Greece and Rome the Renaissance may have discovered, it could not bring to a 'rebirth' their music. Consequently, for want of a classical model on which to be remoulded, this was of all arts the least affected by the Renaissance; and so, like Shakespeare himself, the music of his day tended to be 'behind the times'. At any rate it is possible to choose out from it any number of pieces which lean back towards the Middle Ages,[4] and make an

[4] Pieces by William Byrde and others from the *Fitzwilliam Virginal Book*, for example.

admirably harmonious background to the speeches of Romeo, Lorenzo, Orsino, Ferdinand and others.

These considerations may seem over-subtle, but practically speaking they are important; for if a too purist approach be allowed to forbid a combination of Elizabethan music with medieval dress, our most easily accessible source of suitable music will be barred except on pain of wasp-waists and exaggerated ruffs. But apart from the practical question of what can easily be had, early Tudor[5] and pre-Tudor pieces are no less suitable than Elizabethan ones, and we must remember also that Shakespeare himself had a special love for 'old music'.

All this concerns not merely the songs but above all the incidental music. Shakespeare knew well that some of the most powerful effects of the theatre are gained with the help of music, and he wrote on the understanding that he would be supported when necessary by a marvellous undercurrent of sound, swelling up from time to time into something more than an undercurrent. Medieval and Elizabethan pavanes, galliards, basse danses, branles, measures and the like serve this purpose admirably, for they are just the kind of music that the poet may be supposed to have had in his head when he wrote his plays. Besides, there is a great and growing interest in such music today, no doubt far more than there has been for the last three centuries. How is it, then, that one so rarely has the pleasure of being overwhelmed in the theatre by these *sounds and sweet airs* which blend so wonderfully with the plays, deepening them and being deepened by them, inspiring the actors to excel themselves, and making the audience doubly responsive?[6]

Why so much about music, the reader may ask. Because in considering the different elements which go to make the impact of Shakespeare's plays upon the audience, this particular element, so persistently neglected today as regards both quality and quantity, is of an importance which can scarcely be overestimated.

---

[5] Such as are to be found in Pierre d'Atteignant's early sixteenth-century collection of dances.

[6] A part answer to this question was given by another of our leading theatrical directors, writes: 'I think that most people would prefer to have the music of Shakespeare's time . . . What happens is that when one asks someone to *arrange* the music, he begs so hard to be allowed to *compose* it that the director usually takes the line of least resistance, and gives way.' Whatever the cause, for the last thirty years or more it has been part of the general 'routine' to have a composer for each play just as one has a director and a designer; and when the Old Vic did the complete cycle of Shakespeare's plays, only for two out of the whole thirty-six was the music not specially composed for the production.

> *Therefore the poet*
> *Did feign that Orpheus drew trees, stones and floods*
> *Since naught so stockish, hard, and full of rage,*
> *But music for the time doth change his nature.*
>
> (*The Merchant of Venice*, V, 1)

These last words anticipate our final chapter, for they reflect an acute consciousness, already in the young Shakespeare, of the original and traditional function of music, and therefore, implicitly, of art in its other forms. The true poet is able, through the impact of his plays, to exert such an effect on spectator and reader as *for the time doth change his nature*; and by repetition, with the help of other means, the temporary may become permanent.

CHAPTER 14

THE SECRET

The Western world has been for so long under the spell of humanism, which Edmund personifies in an extreme form, that in some ways we understand the bastard better than we do his legitimate elder brother Edgar, who personifies an outlook which is now very far away. When we are faced with a typical medieval reaction we are sometimes rather at a loss. In *King Lear* the Duke of Albany, hearing that Cornwall has died of a wound he received from a servant when he was putting out Gloster's eyes, says:

> *This shows you are above,*
> *You justicers, that these our nether crimes*
> *So speedily can venge!*   (IV, 2)

and at the end, when he hears of the death of Goneril and Regan, he says:

> *This judgment of the heavens, that makes us tremble,*
> *Touches us not with pity.*

A few moments previously Edgar, referring to his father's sin of adultery, has said to Edmund:

> *The gods are just, and of our pleasant vices*
> *Make instruments to plague us:*
> *The dark and vicious place where thee he got*
> *Cost him his eyes.*

Edmund, whose outlook has been modified by the imminence of death, replies:

Thou has spoken right, 'tis true;
The wheel is come full circle; I am here.

At a cursory reading of the play these speeches are almost embarrassing
to some of us. Our reaction is spontaneously rationalistic. We ask
ourselves what is the meaning of these reiterated assertions that the gods
are just. Can Shakespeare have forgotten for the moment the crying
injustice of Cordelia's death which is just about to become known? Or is
he simply making Edgar and Albany express a rather primitive and
unintelligent point of view which he does not hold himself? The answer
to both questions is certainly 'No'. Our medieval ancestors did not
believe in chance. When a worldly event seemed just, they immediately
recognized the workings of Providence. But their faith remained quite
unruffled in the face of triumphant and prosperous wickedness, for they
knew that any apparent injustices in this world would be made good in
the next. The remarks of Albany and Edgar that I have quoted are simply
spontaneous comments on events, equivalent to some ejaculation such
as 'Laus Deo!' If they jar on us it is because we wrongly suspect an
attempt to justify the ways of God to man. In other words we attribute to
Albany and to Edgar something of a modern psychology, a sort of
primitive rationalism, cruder and less fully developed than our own. We
fail to realize how little store was set in the Middle Ages, despite all their
dialectic, by logical proof.

Shakespeare, unlike Milton, has no illusions about the scope of
reason. He knew that since reason is limited to this world it is powerless
to 'justify the ways of God'. Milton may have known this in theory, but
in practice he was very much a son of the Renaissance, very deeply under the
spell of humanism. *Paradise Lost* cannot be called an intellectual poem.
Milton portrays the next world by sheer force of human imagination.
His God the Father, like Michelangelo's, is fabricated in the image of
man; and the purely logical arguments which he puts into the mouth of
God to justify His ways inevitably fail to convince us. Now Shakespeare
also seeks to justify the ways of God to man. That is, beyond doubt, the
essence of his purpose in writing. But his justification is on an
intellectual plane, where alone it is possible; and this brings us back to
the theme of his plays, for the intellect is none other than the lost faculty
of vision which is symbolized by the Holy Grail and by the Elixir of Life.

In considering how Shakespeare conveys his message to us we must
remember that the true function of art is not didactic. A great drama or
epic may contain little or much teaching of a didactic kind, but it does

not rely on that teaching in order to gain its ultimate effect. Its function
is not so much to define spiritual wisdom as to give us a taste of that
wisdom, each according to his capacity. We may quote in this
connection a profound remark which has been made about sacred art in
Christianity: 'It sets up against the sermon which insists on what must be
done by one who would become holy, a vision of the cosmos which is
holy through its beauty; it makes men participate naturally and almost
involuntarily in the world of holiness.'[1] In its original context it is the
great Norman and Gothic Cathedrals, the sanctuaries in which the
sermon is preached, which immediately spring to mind as examples of
art which reveals a vision of the cosmos. But drama can also yield such a
vision; and to reveal the beauty and thereby the harmony of the universe
is to justify the ways of God.

The first spectators of Shakespeare were probably more receptive
than we are. We tend to take art less seriously than they did. For modern
man the supreme distinction is between 'fiction' and 'truth', as we say,
between art on the one hand and 'reality' on the other. Now naturally
our medieval ancestors made the same distinction, but for them it was
not so sharp. They were not in the habit of speaking and thinking of life
as 'truth'. By truth, by reality, they meant something different; for them
the supreme distinction was not between life and art, but between the
next world, that is, Truth, and this world, which is the shadow of Truth.
The sharpness of that distinction took the edge off all other distinctions.
Moreover, art for them was not merely a copy of life, that is, it was not
merely the shadow of a shadow; it was also by inspiration, partly – and
in some supreme cases even almost wholly – a direct copy or shadow of
the 'substance' itself. The distinction between art and life is therefore
not so much between a shadow and a reality as between two shadows.
This sounds exaggerated, and no doubt the divergence in outlook
between then and now was far slighter for the vast majority than might
appear from what has just been said. But it went certainly further than a
mere verbal quibble over the meaning of the word 'reality', and it would
have been enough to make an appreciable difference in the attitude of an
audience to a play. By attributing a less absolute reality to life they
attributed more reality to art. They no doubt entered into it more
whole-heartedly. But the difference is relative. We also can enter in.
Let us consider what actually happens.

In life we have no view of the whole: we see only bits and pieces here

[1] Titus Burckhardt, *Sacred Art in East and West*. p.46.

and there, and our view is quite distorted. What is near to us we look at
with feverish subjectivity; what is not near we look at with more or less
cold objectivity. Above all we fail to see the pattern. It is as if life were a
great piece of tapestry and as if we looked at it from the wrong side,
where the pattern is obscured by a maze of threads, most of which seem
to have no purpose. Now a play of Shakespeare's is like a much smaller
piece of tapestry, partly copied from the other but also, in virtue of an
aspect of what we call his secret, copied from the transcendent Original
of the other, that Divine Harmony of which the temporal and spatial
cosmos is a reflection, but of which it is merely a reflection, whence the
superficial discords which, for fallen man, give the lie to the profound
beauty of the image as a whole – a totality which he cannot see, being,
by definition, cut off from the vision of it. The remarkable intensity of
Shakespeare's copy is redoubled by the corresponding intensity of those
who hear it and see it. The dramatist is highly privileged with a privilege
that he shares with no other artist, except the composer of music,
namely the extreme passivity of his audience. It is in the nature of things
that people go to a play in the hope that they will be spellbound.
Shakespeare holds out this smaller piece of tapestry to us in the theatre,
between ourselves and him. He is on the right side of it and we are again
on the wrong side just as, unlike him, we are on the wrong side of the
great tapestry of life. To begin with we look at the rather chaotic maze of
threads with the same cold objectivity with which we view the threads of
our neighbours' lives. But little by little, as the play goes on, we are
drawn into it and become more and more bound up with its threads.
Our cold objectivity vanishes and we feel the warmth of subjectivity. So
it is with any dramatic piece, one may say. That is true; but with most
drama what is the benefit to be gained? It is simply a question of
exchanging one's ordinary subjectivity for another one which is no
better and which may be worse. But when a drama is created as an image
of the whole universe, and when the hero represents a great soul which
is being purified of all its faults, and being developed towards the limits
of human possibility, then it is no light thing to be drawn into the web of
the tapestry and to become identified with its central figure. But that is
not all: the purification of the hero is in view of an end. By the close of
the play we have become objective once more, but with a higher
objectivity which is completely different from the initial one; for
Shakespeare has drawn us right through the tapestry and out at the other
side, so that we now see it as it really is, a unity in which all the parts fit
marvellously together to make up a perfect whole. Having been given a

taste of the hero's purification we are now given one of the spiritual wisdom to which it leads: and just as Shakespeare's small tapestry merges mysteriously with the great tapestry of life, so our view of the harmony and beauty of the one is also, in a sense, a view of the harmony and beauty of the other. We 'participate naturally and almost involuntarily in the world of holiness'. It is only a momentary glimpse, and it does not last. But it none the less makes an imprint upon the soul, which may not be easily effaced.

Shakespeare's being from the outset on the right side of the small tapestry he holds out to us in the theatre is part of his secret as an artist; his being on the right side of the great tapestry of life is part of his secret as a man. This higher objectivity is directly mentioned by King Lear at the beginning of the last scene of the play. He is now almost at the end of the quest, and he imagines what it would mean to be altogether united with Cordelia who, according to the deeper meaning of the play, is herself a personification of the same objectivity which can, to use her own words,

outfrown false fortune's frown.

In an already quoted speech, the King says that they will live together in prison

> *And pray, and sing, and tell old tales, and laugh*
> *At gilded butterflies, and hear poor rogues*
> *Talk of court news; and we'll talk with them too,*
> *Who loses and who wins; who's in, who's out;*
> *And take upon's the mystery of things*
> *As if we were God's spies.*   (V,3)

Alone the eye of the intellect, the eye of the angels who are *God's spies*, can perceive the justice of the workings of Providence. It is clearly from the standpoint of this higher objectivity that the maturer plays were written; and when at the end, having passed through the tapestry, we stand side by side with Shakespeare himself, we also for the moment have in a sense taken upon ourselves *the mystery of things*.

Let us consider this in a slightly different way. The fall of man is represented traditionally as the acquisition of the knowledge of good and evil. The intellectual knowledge of Absolute Good is lost and is replaced by a purely mental knowledge which is only capable of grasping a relative good, that good which is the opposite of evil. We have thus the illusion that the devil is the opposite of God, whereas in reality nothing at all can stand in the scales against Divine Providence. In the course of *Othello*, for example, as also in the course of *King Lear*, Shakespeare has shown us the extremities of relative good and evil; but by the end it is as if for the moment he has taken out of our mouths the taste of the fruit of the Forbidden Tree. The knowledge of good and evil is there, but it no longer blinds us to the Absolute Good. We no longer ask ourselves that most difficult of all questions 'Why does God allow evil?' for we have mysteriously felt the answer to it, where alone the answer lies, upon the plane of the intellect. We accept everything with serenity and would change nothing. We feel in an inexplicable way that all is well, not according to human justice which in any case is fragmentary, being largely based on ignorance, but according to 'poetic justice', which is none other than Divine Justice. But it is not only sorrow that can work this wonder in us: just as we accept the endings of *Othello* and *King Lear*, so also we accept the endings of *Cymbeline* and *The Winter's Tale*. It is not the same with the happy endings of *Twelfth Night* and *As You Like It*, for example. Nor is the total effect of *Romeo and Juliet* comparable to that of the great tragedies. The best of the pre-*Hamlet* plays, *Romeo and Juliet* and *A Midsummer Night's Dream* included, have a total effect of undeniably exalting and peace-giving harmony, but this is something less transcendent than the harmony of the Universe itself, nor can it come near to making us forget 'the knowledge of good and evil' or to justifying the ways of God.

But once he has succeeded in justifying those ways, Shakespeare does so not only once but again and again, which suggests that his own life was patterned upon the pattern of his plays, and that he was writing about what he himself knew. There is nothing really extravagant in such a claim, for according to the traditional conception of poetry, a poet should be no less than a seer, *vates*; and the Garden of Helicon, the abode of Apollo and the Muses, the only source of true poetic inspiration, is as Dante tells us none other than the Garden of Eden, where grows the Tree of Life whose fruit is the only antidote to the poison of the knowledge of good and evil.

Always allowing that there are many different degrees of being inspired, the explanation of what Shakespeare is able to do to us can only lie in his inspiration or, if one prefers it, in his intellectuality, which according to the true sense of the word really amounts to the same. It is certainly not a mere question of the power of language, neither is it merely a question of the feelings of pity and terror, as might be concluded from Aristotle's all too inexplicit references to catharsis. The verse of Webster's *Duchess of Malfi* is fine enough, like that of Shelley's

Cenci; nor are the elements of pity and terror lacking, to say the least. Yet these two plays leave us rather with feelings of horror than with visionary acceptance and serenity. The key to what Aristotle meant by catharsis lies above all in the example he gives, and it is clear from this that the 'purification' in question is no less than what has been described here in other terms, for the effect upon us of Sophocles' *Oedipus* is in fact essentially the same as that of *King Lear*.

Many secondary features of Shakespeare's plays suggest that the poet had power to draw upon the transcendent. Characters like Hamlet and Cleopatra for example are not so much fabrications as 'creations'. There is something almost miraculously alive about them as if they had been brought down ready made from above. An analogous remark could be made about his coining of words.[2] Created also rather than fabricated are the worlds in which the plays are set: each is like a unique sphere of existence with its own atmosphere which makes it quite distinct from all the other Shakespearean macrocosms. But contact with a transcendent source is above all suggested by the constant repetition of a transcendent total effect. That contact is a secret, for it belongs to the domain of the Mysteries; but the true and original purpose of art – the primal reason for its existence – is precisely to communicate secrets, not by blurting them out but by offering them as it were with half open hand, by bringing them near and inviting us to approach.

It is generally agreed that in *The Tempest*, Prospero's magic, aside from its other meanings, is intended to represent Shakespeare's own powers as an artist; and truly inspired art is indeed a kind of white magic which casts a spell over man and momentarily changes him, doing as it were the impossible and making him quite literally excel himself.

[2] See p.66 note 9.

INDEX